TABLE OF CONTENT

ARTISTS & CRAFTSWOMEN

FEMINIST THEATRE

DANCE

WOMYN'S MUSIC FESTIVALS

INTERVIEW

OBITUARIES

NOTES FOR A MAGAZINE

*S*inister Wisdom 104: *Lesbianima Rising* is the third collection of stories from the Southern Lesbian Feminist Activist Oral Herstory Project. I am thrilled to present this issue and to be working with the phenomenal women involved in this project.

Of course, this work appeals to me as a historian interested in lesbian lives during the twentieth century. It addresses gaps in contemporary historiography which too often ignores the south and activism of women not recognized or embraced by key leaders in the coastal United States. By centering the lives of southern women, we can reimagine and develop new understandings of lesbian lives in the US—and, I hope, in other global locations.

Yet, this work is not only about history. *Sinister Wisdom* 104: *Lesbianima Rising* explores the power of music, art, craft, theatre, dance, and festival gatherings in women's lives. It complements the last issue *Sinister Wisdom* 103: *Celebrating the Michigan Womyn's Music Festival* as well as the two previous issues from the Southern Lesbian Feminist Activist Oral Herstory Project, *Sinister Wisdom* 93 and *Sinister Wisdom* 98. Collectively, these issues—and all of the issues of *Sinister Wisdom*—build a foundation, intellectually, politically, and culturally—to ignite our futures.

By documenting and analyzing a vibrant lesbian-feminist past, we create vehicles for women to imagine new futures and to have tools, maps, inspirations, and stories to create new futures for lesbians and feminists. All of this work could not be more important in the time of the Trump Presidency in the US and while other movements of nationalism and populism blossom around the world. Our work to nurture lesbian communities and lift up lesbian lives is a crucial mode of resistance. Culture, particularly lesbian art and culture, challenges narratives of domination with new visions for the world.

In addition to the work of the Southern Lesbian Feminist Activist Oral Herstory Project, *Sinister Wisdom* 104: *Lesbianima Rising* contains a fascinating interview by Sandra Tarlin with nonagenarian poet Naomi Replansky and Joan Nestle's reflections on Replansky's *Collected Poems*. This issue also carries a number of obituaries, including one for long-time *Sinister Wisdom* volunteer and administrator Susan Levinkind. Losing Susan has been very sad for me and for *Sinister Wisdom*. Susan's good spirits, practical advice and hours and hours of work made *Sinister Wisdom* vibrant and sustainable during years when lesbian organizations foundered. Her memory is a blessing to us all.

Finally, support for our fall fundraising campaign in 2016 was extraordinary and subscriptions are growing! I continued to be awed and humbled by lesbians' support for *Sinister Wisdom*.

In sisterhood,

Julie R Enszer
April 2017

SINISTER WISDOM FALL FUNDRAISING CAMPAIGN ACKNOWLEDGEMENTS

Thank you to all of the supporters of the *Sinister Wisdom* fall fundraising campaign! We raised over $5,500 to support *Sinister Wisdom* during 2017. Thank you to all of our fall fundraising campaign supporters and subscribers listed below.

A G Brigham
Alice Bloch
Alice Hom
Amanda Bloom
Amy Brigham
Andrea Clark
Ann Powers
Anne Fairbrother
Anne Goldstein
Anne Habel
Barbara Ester
Bernice Lee
Beth Hodges
Beth Sommers
Bette Rosenthal
Billie Parish
Bridget Dorward
Brittany Lewis
Bryan Borland & Sibling Rivalry Press llc
Carol Anne Douglas
Carol R Rosenfeld
Carole Friesen
Carole Powell
Carolyn D'Cruz
Carrie J Devall
Casey Parnis
Charlene Senn
Cheryl Clarke
Chocolate Waters
Christina Reitz
Clare Coss
Connie Tarpley
Cordelia Strandskov
Cristina Vegas
Dawn Smith

Debra Cummings
Denise Duhamel
Denise E Dedman
Diane Furtney
Diane P Gallagher
Dolphin Dragon
Donna Fletcher
doris davenport
Editorial Rx, Inc
Elise Chenier
Emily Dziuban
Evelyn Beck
Gail Ludwig
Gail Suber
Gillian P Herbert
J B
J B Kerr / Wendy Webster
Jaime L Harker
Jan Griesinger
Jane Nichols
Jane Meyerding
Jayne Snook
Jean Frances
Jeanne Lupton
Jemma T Crae
Jendi Reiter
Jennifer Oliveri
Jenny Factor
Jill F Anania
Jo Oppenheimer
Jo Kenny & Gloria Nieto
Joan Larkin
Joan Moore
Joan Nestle
Jody Jewdyke
Judith A Reagan

Judith Witherow
& Sue Lenaerts
Justine Hernandez
Kae Bell
Karen L Erlichman
Karin Kratz
Kathleen Carey
Kaye Paton
Kelsey Moody
Kl Abshier
Laura Rifkin
Laura X
Lena Rothman
Lillian Donovan
Linda Cuellar
Linda J Bassham
Linda Stein
Linda Watskin
Lisa Dordal
Lisa J Hernandez
Lisa Szer
Liz Ahl
Liz Minette
Lori Hirtelen
Lucy Bledsoe
Lynette Yetter
Lynn Johnson
Lynne Phoenix
Maggie A Schleich
Marcy Wilder
Mardi Steinau
Maria DeGuzman
Maria Molina
Marie Steinwachs
Marilyn Mesh
Martha Ertman

Martha Nell Smith
Martha Pillow
Mary Donnelly
Mary Ellen Rico
Mary Garcia
Mary McClintock
Maureen T Seaton
Megan Behrent
Megan Welsh
Melinda A Szell
Merran B Newman
Merril Mushroom
Michael K Markus
Michele Sigl
Miriam Frank
Morgan Pharis
Ms. Flint
Myriam Fougere
NA Tilsen
Nan Worthing
Nicola Griffith
Noreen Rapp
Pamela Mayberry
Pat Hulsebosch
Patricia Bryan
Patricia Cull

Patricia E Barry
Priscella B Bellairs
Rachel . Pray
Rebeka Hoffman
Regina & Irene Dick-Endrizzi
Rena Carney
Roberta Arnold
Roberta Pato
Robin Becker
Ronald W Mohring
Ronda Medors
Ronna Jo Magy
Rose L Norman
Ruth Berman
Ruth Hooper
Sally Stranquist
Sandra L Covahey
Sandra Mattson
Sandra Thornby
Sandy Tate
Sara Karon
Sarah Browning
Sarah Carroll
Sarah Rauber
Sarah Schulman
Sarah Valentine

Sharon Parnell
Shellyse M Szakacs
Sherry Cmiel
Shylo Wood & Redtail
Sonia Lopez
Stephanie Schroeder
Sue Lenaerts
Susan E. Wiseheart
Susan McCullough
Susan Wiseheart
Susie Kisber PhD
Syndy Sharp
Tara Shea Burke
Teja Oblak
TeNaj McFadden
Teresa Muniz
Theresa Varela
Toni Fitzpatrick
Trish Devine
Tryna Hope
Valerie Wetlaufer
Viviane Morrigan
Wendy Judith Cutler
Yasmin Tambiah

Error in listing? Name missing? I apologize for any errors. Please bring it to my attention at julie@sinisterwisdom.org so that I can correct it immediately.

If you missed the *Sinister Wisdom* fall fundraising campaign, make a gift online at www.SinisterWisdom.org.

NOTES FOR A SPECIAL ISSUE

It is easy to become absorbed in one's art. Easy to become absorbed in the process of creating, in the audience response, the business (especially when profits are few). It is easy to forget those who make women's art and music happen. Those who work long hours for little or no money, to bring women's culture to you. If we are to survive as a culture, as a community, we will acknowledge and value each other's contributions. If we don't acknowledge each other, I am afraid no one else will.

B eth York spoke these words to introduce her 1986 concert at the Unitarian Church of Atlanta, GA. They seem particularly relevant to introduce this special edition of *Sinister Wisdom*, devoted to the creative arts during a time of lesbian feminist activism in the 1970s, 1980s, and 1990s. The words are relevant in that they establish our intention with this edition to acknowledge Southern lesbian and women's artistic activities during a timeframe when the arts were becoming an integral part of lesbian feminist activism nationwide, and especially in urban areas. The South was no exception, even though Southern lesbian feminist artistic life has largely been omitted from existing texts on the topic.[1] A notable exception is an excellent article on the Gulf Coast Women's Music Festival and the inclusion of other Southern women's music festivals in Bonnie Morris' *Eden Built by Eves* (1999). Morris also recognized Ladyslipper Music in Durham, NC, as they worked to promote and market less famous artists.

---

1 For example, *Women's Culture in a New Era: A Feminist Revolution?* ed. Gayle Kimball (Lanham, MD: Scarecrow Press, 2005).

The role of the arts in building lesbian community and providing venues for social activism was inevitable, given the political and social fervor of the times. In the way that the civil rights movement produced songs and cultural events that supported ending discrimination against African Americans, so did the feminist movement spark empowered lesbian artists to produce their own cultural events, recordings, and distribution outlets. A woman-identified consciousness supported this culture, both spiritually and financially.[2] Art was informed by feminist ideals carried by the artists, poets, performers, and playwrights, and interwoven into production companies, recording companies, arts organizations, and into the art itself.

Some have insisted that women's arts and cultural activities were integral to the political aims of the feminist movement. Others criticized that so-called "cultural feminism" co-opted or distracted from feminist political activism.[3] The editors of this edition assume the former stance. Our experience of women-only (and in some cases, lesbian-only) cultural events and activities was that they provided opportunities to communicate, to transmit feminist values, to network, and to experience each other's creativity. Southern lesbian visual artists, musicians, actors, dancers, poets, and writers were seen and heard in safe spaces where they openly presented new and often political works. A lesbian dancer, painter, composer, or craftswomon, informed by lesbian feminist politic, was free to create intentional venues for her works to be shown for their own sake, even without overtly political context. As in other parts of the United States, the Southern lesbian (and gay) choral movement drew large local audiences in Tampa, Atlanta, and Richmond, and gave voice to community singers who might never have had the opportunity to perform. Grassroots organizations located in the South produced,

---

2   Ruth Scovill, "Women's Music" in *Women's Culture: Renaissance of the Seventies,* ed. Gayle Kimball (Metuchen, NJ: Scarecrow Press, 1981), pp.148–62.

3   Alice Echols, *Daring to Be Bad: Radical Feminism in America, 1967-1975* (Minneapolis: University of Minnesota Press, 1989).

distributed, and marketed recordings and concerts by lesbian musicians, both local and nationally known artists.

The Southern lesbian writers of Womonwrites have once again collected writings for a third special edition of *Sinister Wisdom*. The works presented here are derived from direct solicitations, interviews, and previously written articles that have been submitted and collaboratively edited by Womonwriters. All of the interviews referenced here are archived in full (audio and interview notes) in the Sallie Bingham Center for Women's History and Culture in the Rubenstein Rare Book & Manuscript Library at Duke University. The pieces in this issue are snapshots, serving as mere reflections of the breadth and scope of Southern artistic activity within our timeframe, generally from the early 1970s to the mid-1990s. Ironically, a limitation of this edition is that the editors had so much material that it necessitated making hard editing decisions. In an attempt to be comprehensive, we have material for a textbook on the topic, and have saved more than half of our writings for what we hope will be more special issues. That includes all materials about the kind of lesbian-feminist creative writing and writing groups that have sustained Womonwrites since 1979. We also acknowledge that during the years of our timeline, the integration of White lesbian culture into Black lesbian "womonism" in the South was an ideal, although not easy to actualize. We have done our best to bring the voices of women of color onto these pages and realize there is always more work to be done.

What you will not see in *Sinister Wisdom* 104: *Lesbianima Rising* are articles on Southern lesbian artists who have achieved fame within the lesbian and/or mainstream popular culture. Meg Christian was born in North Carolina, but she is famous in older lesbian circles and moved from the South to become one of the first singer-songwriters produced by Olivia Records. Bernice Johnson Reagon was born near Albany, GA, but Sweet Honey in the Rock, the a cappella vocal ensemble she formed in 1971, has achieved international acclaim and is not represented in this edition. But you may not know about Sisters of No Mercy, Anima Rising, Lofty Notions, Yer Girlfriend, Red Dyke Theatre, and Pagoda Playhouse. They are among the unsung sheros of lesbian Southern arts who also deserve to be documented and acknowledged for their work in building vibrant Southern lesbian communities.

We hope that you will absorb yourself in this rich tapestry of Southern stories and reflections on the creative arts. We hope that they will bring back your own memories of lesbian dances, concerts, exhibits, book signings, and images of our arts and culture, and remind you of the meaning, beauty, emotional expression, imagination, and core feminist values contained in their works. We especially thank Julie Enszer, the *Sinister Wisdom* editors and Board of Directors, and the Womonwriters for their support of this project.

Beth York
Merril Mushroom
Rose Norman

MEL

Rand Hall

"Are you Melody or Melanie or Melissa maybe?"

In the back of a crowded bar the darkened stage is an oasis of silence. Mikes and guitars wait for electric life.

Mel steps behind her drums
settles her slim hips on the stool
a driver in the seat
of an eighteen-wheeler

eyes eager with anticipation
looking out into the night
watching for the cue
to hit overdrive

ten forward speeds and no reverse
the flying sticks gripped
in leather gloves beat the song
through the smoky air

sneakered foot
beats the base like a snare
fueled by coke and demons all her own
she's racing the rhythm of the night

off
on a solitary ride

for Melody Givans
December 30, 1951, to March 25, 2005

Photo by Rand Hall

Mel played with Leslie Kyle in several rebirths of the lesbian band Buffalo Shoes during the 1980s in the Tampa and St. Pete, Florida area. The photo was taken of Mel with Silk Heat at The Cheshire Cat in Gulfport, FL.

CONSCIOUSNESS-RAISING WITH ANIMA RISING

Beth York

Coming out as a lesbian feminist was intimately linked to the vibrant lesbian-feminist cultural movement that had taken root when I moved to Atlanta in 1977. A naïve young folk singer at twenty-seven, I had finally admitted my attractions to women. Earlier, in 1973–74, as a hetero newlywed, I became a member of a consciousness-raising (CR) group for six months in California while completing a clinical internship in music therapy. There I attended my first "women-only" gathering. Somewhere in the forests of northern California, our group consumed organic food prepared and served by strong women in jeans and soft flannel shirts. I saw my vulva and cervix for the first time, up-close and personal, with mirror, flashlight, and plastic speculum. I heard Margie Adam sing and speak about a new women's music movement. Women's music . . . hmmm. I am a woman, a folksinger, a musician. I am beginning to write original songs. Sounds like me. I had listened and learned from recordings of Joan Baez, Judy Collins, Joni Mitchell, Laura Nyro, and Carole King since I was fourteen. I tucked the term "women's music" in my back pocket for future reference. Meanwhile, I was challenged in our weekly CR group and excited by what I heard. My eyes opened to the injustices women faced, injustices inherent in traditional roles that I had never questioned. I hadn't considered an alternative to marrying that sweet hippie boy I had held onto for the last ten years. I listened to each woman's story and was moved by our common concerns. I was also intellectually—and otherwise—stimulated.

After my internship, Dave and I moved back South to Athens, GA, where we rented a room in a large Victorian house on Bloomfield Street, inhabited mostly by radical lesbians living near the University of Georgia. Dave took care of some badly needed repairs to the house. I worked part-time and was immediately drawn into intense late-night conversations and continued CR with Deb, Pat, Carol, Anastasia, and Leslie.

Deb was a theatre major with a mischievous smile and unbounded energy. We flirted. She dressed me for my folksinger gigs at the B&B Warehouse. I loved her attention. Finally we kissed. Not long afterward, Kay, the organizer of the California CR group, moved across country to live with us at the Bloomfield house. One afternoon she became my first woman lover. We seduced each other with wine and deep talks "up on the roof" outside her second-story room.

Dave had outside love interests as well. This was the 1970s. We were questioning everything, including traditional marriage. What was this marriage anyway? We were definitely *not* monogamous. My relationships with these women were becoming more important to me than him, and finally I told him so. He was not concerned. They were only women, he said. I was furious. He had inadvertently admitted that women were not as important as men. What did that say about our marriage? I breathed a sigh of relief. My consciousness had been raised, the personal *was* political. I was getting stronger. I would be divorcing him soon.

My next memory is attending a conference of the National Organization for Women in Athens, hearing Gloria Steinem, and performing at a lesbian "alternative" event (where all my new friends seemed to be). I was ready to pursue the next course in my lesbian-feminist education, to make the paradigm shift from male identification to woman identification. I returned from a summer course in jazz at the Berklee College of Music in Boston in the summer of 1975 and filed for divorce. By that time, I had found comfort with three women on Bloomfield Street. Women were my first priority. I moved to Atlanta.

Atlanta opened her doors wide onto my new life. Her symbol was the Phoenix rising from the ashes, and my changes felt as profound as the image of that fiery bird. By day, I worked as a music therapist at the Georgia Mental Health Institute. Several nurses and therapists who worked with me were "out" lesbians. They introduced me to happy hour at the Tower and Ms. Garbo's, two very different lesbian bars, one working class, and the other a little more upscale. Charis Books and More was down the street on Moreland Avenue—"more" being more feminist literature than I had ever dreamed of—and a community bulletin board advertising all the events in and around the Little Five Points/Candler Park area where I lived.

By 1975, Lucina's Music had formed, the new lesbian-feminist production company, founded by ten members from the Atlanta Lesbian Feminist Alliance (ALFA). According to their charter,

> Ten women have banded together in Atalanta, the city of the self-resurrecting Phoenix. We call ourselves Lucina's Music, invoking Her name and strengths. We felt the void in this city, and we are working to let womn's voices be heard. We have committed ourselves to the production and propagation of Womn's Music and Culture.[1]

The "Artist's Introduction" to the new production company read:

> Women Make Music: We are singing, playing and composing works about the things which touch women's lives. All too often, however, these efforts are denigrated, ignored, and kept under control by the male-dominated music industry. That leaden hand has exercised a powerful grasp upon the throat of women's creativity. But rather than obligingly being throttled, women's music across the land is stirring, strengthening, and growing. Small ruptures and attempts to loosen the stranglehold appear—an artist here, an independent record there. . . . This movement is gathering voice, as women set up record companies, distribution systems, and production groups to develop women's music.

---

1 ALFA Archives, Box 24, Sallie Bingham Center for Women's History and Culture in the Rubenstein Rare Book & Manuscript Library at Duke University.

Happily, this phenomenon is not erupting just in other parts of the country. Atlanta is now beginning to shake off its own heavy hand, becoming more receptive to female artists. This city has never been the most hospitable provider to gain any exposure for their work. Yet, a substantial audience exists in Atlanta for female artists who play and sing about women's concerns. The problem revolves around getting the artist and audience together.

Last fall, a group of ten area women decided to expedite matters. Thus, an all-woman concert production group came into being. We have emerged as producers dedicated to providing, promoting, and nurturing music by Atlanta women, for Atlanta women.

We call ourselves Lucina's Music, after the light-bearing Goddess who created all the civilizing arts (especially music). She seems to smile on our endeavors....[2]

Fast forward...1978. A psychiatric nurse at Georgia Mental Health told me about a women's coffeehouse where I could perform at the Little Five Points Pub. It was sponsored by Lucina's Music. Elizabeth, a local poet, was reading her work. A lesbian was singing original songs. I auditioned at the ALFA House, and the women who I auditioned for agreed to let me on stage. That night I sang Joan Baez, Judy Collins, and Joni Mitchell songs, sported wild Janis Joplin hair, and wore a purple-flowered dress. I tried my best to look like, sing like many of the women I admired, . . . but I don't remember any of the other women in the audience wearing a dress. Most of them were wearing blue jeans and those soft flannel shirts.

Later, I heard about an ALFA party at the house on McClendon. I mustered up the courage and decided to take myself there. A respectable source reports that I flew into the ALFA House, long hair flying, and headed straight for the piano at the other side

---

2 *Ibid.*

of the room. (I believe I wore jeans that day.) It was easy to hide behind the piano keys. I decided to play background music, and accompany these women and their important conversations. These were *real* lesbians, after all, tall, strong, butch and brash, smart and political. I envied their spitfire confidence, intellect, and easy sexuality. I, on the other hand, was shy and femme-looking. Music was the best way to connect. Music is, after all, vibrational, magnetic energy. These women would be attracted to my music making. If I played, I reasoned, eventually one of these women would come to *me*.

My strategy worked. Eventually, a strong, fine woman approached the piano; we exchanged smiles, names, pleasantries. I stopped playing to talk to her. Her name was Phyllis, and she was a drummer—a drummer—I had only met one other woman drummer. She wanted to start a woman's band. Would I be interested? The invitation was perfectly timed. I made my way OUT and IN to the bourgeoning Atlanta lesbian community.

In the midst of this lesbian-feminist cultural uprising centered at the ALFA house, our band was born: Her name was "Anima Rising." The name came from an old Joni Mitchell song. The "feminine aspect of the divine" was rising—akin to that phoenix rising from the ashes—and our aspirations of making it in the music business rose as well. Soon after Phyllis and I met, KC (on bass) and Jan (guitar, flute, with a voice like a country diva) joined us. We were all songwriters, wearing our own unique styles and egos. Jan was a counselor at the mental health center where I worked. She was biding her time, saving her money so that she could go mainstream with her music. Her ultimate goal was to win a Grammy Award. KC was the youngest, a political radical, opinionated poet who wrote a regular column for *Southern Voice*, the Atlanta gay/lesbian newspaper. I was discovering jazz, and had started to play piano and hotel gigs around Atlanta. Phyllis played rock and roll to jazz to, well, *anything*.

We began to rehearse when a mutual friend, Marsha June, opened up her living room to us. At least twice a week we rehearsed there, our music peppered with marijuana, political discussions, and dreams of becoming Women's Music Stars. We had heard

Photo courtesy of Beth York

Beth York performing with Anima Rising at the Pagoda in 1979.

about Olivia Records, Cris Williamson's *Changer and the Changed*, and Meg Christian's *I Know You Know*. We sent a demo tape to pianist and songwriter Margie Adam, who kindly wrote us back and urged us to continue.

We performed all around Atlanta. Ms. Garbo's was a regular gig, a smoke-filled women's bar on Cheshire Bridge Road with an established clientele. Our music wasn't exactly the dance music of the time. We were performing original, sometimes political songs, songs with a message, songs about loving women. "Ain't I a Woman" was one of Phyllis' songs, inspired by Sojourner Truth. We followed Margie, Meg, Cris and Kay Gardner, and the growing national women's music scene. We expanded our performances to more gay- and women-centered performance venues: the Little Five Points Pub, Georgia State University Women's Center, the Pagoda in St. Augustine, Atlanta Pride, and Little Five Points community celebrations. We performed at benefits for ALFA, WRFG, and the Karuna Counseling Collective. We opened for Medusa, a duo consisting of Flash Silvermoon and her partner Pan. We were going places and *fast*. In the meantime, Lucina's was producing Meg Christian, Margie Adam, Terese Edell, Linda Tillery, and Mary Watkins.

We were also on the bill for another Lucina's Music coffeehouse at the Phoenix Fellowship, January 20, 1979, "childcare and work exchange" provided. That night we shared the stage with nationally known women's music artists, Betsy Rose and Cathy Winter. Sandra Franks presented a one-woman performance portraying Harriet Tubman that night. The room was packed, and the crowd was rowdy and supportive. We were sounding good. On January 31, 1979, I wrote in my journal:

> Our music emerges from a variety of experiences
> Anger from our oppression
> Sorrow at being misunderstood
> Strength and joy in discovery
> In an atmosphere of creative acceptance

Where minds and hearts
Wrestle and toil
Emerge with a fresh perspective,
Perhaps a new song
The totality of our individual experience
Comprises the whole
Of who we are as women.

In March of that year, Phyllis and I approached the women of Lucina's Music with a grand proposal for a women's music center. They listened politely and suggested a "separate structure and bylaws," but agreed to sponsorship. We could create our own space, our own support network and umbrella for other organizations devoted to women's music. We did not follow-through. We were too busy performing to create a new organization!

We weren't the only local lesbian musicians performing in Atlanta at the time. Fonda and Dede and Pretty Good for Girls played jazz at upscale clubs in Buckhead. Dede was an excellent bassist, arranger, and singer-songwriter. Fonda played a mean jazz piano, as did Penelope, who was a traditionally beautiful solo artist. The Fabulous Scallion Sisters was Dede's other band. The difference between those artists and Anima Rising was that the messages in our music conveyed a lesbian-feminist point of view. We were happy and comfortable in all lesbian and women's audiences. Gail Reeder and Sisters of No Mercy were even more radical than we were, even though some of those players were straight. But we were all women making music, at varying levels of radicalism, feminist consciousness, and "outwardness."

Reviews were positive. One Atlanta music critic wrote, "Each member of Anima Rising is a qualified musician in her own right. Put them all together on stage and the result is slick—tight musicianship and strong, clear vocals."[3] Another wrote that the band had "slick rhythms and smooth lyrics about changes in life,

---

3   M. Lampe, "Atlanta's Women are Anima Rising." *Signal*, Georgia State University, March 4, 1980, p. 29.

looking for love, and feeling happy. . . . Although the band is not OVERTLY feminist, the fact that all the musicians are *women* does, and should, influence their music..."[4] The critic continued, "Members like Phyllis Free, 'simply got tired of playing supporting roles to further some male musician's career.' Anima Rising is a cooperative outfit that provides an outlet for the band members' talents. Each woman is a writer, and the band strives to create a blend of all five different styles."[5] That was an understatement.

"Strives to create" was an operative ideal. What we began to discover was that not all of us equally embraced lesbian-feminist politics. Not all of us wanted to make a political statement through our lyrics. It was hard to make a living as a musician and keep lofty ideals intact. We kept our day jobs. We hadn't hired a manager to find regular bookings and we certainly weren't ready to take a leap of faith and go on the road. Negotiating contracts was not our forte, and the venues that were a good fit for our music were few and far between. We didn't have enough original material to make a studio recording—and besides, we didn't have the money to book studio time. Ladyslipper Music, the new women's music catalog and distribution company in Durham, NC, was not knocking at our door—and we weren't ready to knock on theirs.

Disgruntlement set in as we debated what our next step should be. Should we branch out and perform cover tunes so that we could sign on with a manager and pursue club work? That would mean a commitment to making music our livelihood, and we just didn't feel ready. Meanwhile, one night, as Anima Rising was playing in Athens, GA, I introduced the band members to our opening act, an Athens friend who was also a singer-songwriter. Jan R was a soloist who was booking herself on the Holiday Inn route to fame and glory—affectionately known as the "chittlin' circuit." She played and sang cover tunes and originals that had a swinging, easy

---

4 *Ibid.*

5 *Ibid.*

sound. She had a good business head. She was easy to connect with. So easy that Phyllis fell for Jan. And Jan fell for Phyllis. And Jan began to rehearse with us at Marsha June's place.

Jan was sweet and seductive in a femme, hippie sort of way. She joined us for a few performances, and afterwards, in our conversations during rehearsals, began to mention her own gigs. She wondered if any of us would join her. We could keep Anima Rising intact, but a new band, Jan R and Friends, would enable those of us who wanted to play more regularly to quit our jobs and hit the road. Phyllis was ready; I was ready to discharge myself from the mental health center and leave Atlanta to seek fame and fortune. Off we went, believing we could be true to both bands. After all, as feminists, we had questioned monogamy as a patriarchal construct. Jan, Phyllis, and I played as a trio in Gainesville, FL, in Arabi, GA, in Chattanooga, TN, and our favorite, Hilton Head Island where—as fate would have it—Phyllis fell in love again, this time with the tennis pro at the resort where we were booked.

When we finally made it back to Atlanta, it was clear to Anima Rising—and Jan R and Friends—that we would be left waiting as Phyllis departed to live on Hilton Head Island. Ironically, in July of 1980, a journalist had just written a rave review and article about Anima Rising—with a picture of all of us—Jan R included—in the upscale *Atlanta Magazine*: "They take the stage like any band: high-stepping over wires, strapping on guitars, noodling to check sound levels. But when the lights come up and they face the audience with their first chord, it's not business as usual. The five players are all women."[6] Anima Rising's final shows in 1980 were performances at Womonwrites, the lesbian writers retreat, and the closing of Ms. Garbo's bar. KC asserted, "Playing original music means that we're playing ourselves, and we're singing

---

6 Patricia Thompson, "On The Cusp With Anima Rising," *Atlanta Magazine* 20:3 (July 1980): 27.

ourselves." For those three years, we sang ourselves fiercely, proudly, beautifully.

Anima Rising publicity photo, Atlanta, GA, 1979.

RIVER CITY WIMMIN

Joyce Hopkins

In the mid-1970s, key features of the lesbian community in Louisville included both feminism and separatism, that is, minimizing or avoiding interaction with men, either gay or straight. That gave rise to the Lesbian Feminist Union, some of whose members pooled expertise and financial resources to incorporate and create Mother's Brew, up a steep set of stairs at 204 W. Market Street in Louisville. As a women-only bar and gathering space, Mother's Brew was unique in Kentucky (possibly in the South), providing an emotional anchor in an era when lesbians regularly lost their homes, their jobs, and their children because of their sexuality.

The beating heart of Mother's Brew was River City Wimmin, the four-woman house band consisting of Teresa Davis, Joyce Hopkins, Bettie Keeling, and Marge VanGilder. Their covers were

Photo courtesy of Joyce Hopkins

River City Wimmin in 1977 or 1978 (l to r): Joyce Hopkins,
Teresa Davis, Bettie Keeling, Marge VanGilder.

exciting, and their vocal harmonies flawless, but their greatest gift to the lesbian community was their embodiment of female strength, determination, and good humor. While the breakup of River City Wimmin in 1978 spelled the beginning of the end for Mother's Brew (which closed in 1979), Hopkins, Keeling, and VanGilder soon reunited, first as River City Wimmin and later as Tiffany. No longer reliant on separatism and a "captive" lesbian audience, they courageously took their energy into the larger world and established that lesbian women could be both independent and successful. As VanGilder observed, "Just the fact that there are three women musicians onstage, with no man present, is a feminist statement." Throughout the 1980s, Tiffany inspired and encouraged local lesbian musicians, and they were in constant demand for birthday, holiday, and anniversary parties in the gay and lesbian community.

YER GIRLFRIEND:
LOUISVILLE'S COMMUNITY BAND, 1989–96
LauRose Dancingfire Felicity and Calla Felicity

"**W**e won't be silent!" was the theme of the first album of the band that became Louisville's lesbian community band from 1989 to 1996, with reunion concerts as recently as 2016. In the seven or eight years of their existence, they became Louisville's community band, a band whose main goal was to serve the lesbian community in Louisville. It was a community that also supported the band, following them to festivals and to concerts in other Kentucky cities, as well as in neighboring states. They played mostly in the Southeast but, as their fan base grew, so did their territory—from Milwaukee to New Orleans, from Key West to Provincetown, and at many lesbian festivals and events in between. They were always ready to play a benefit for an LGBTQ event, and became the soundtrack for Louisville's Fairness Campaign, which began seeking antidiscrimination protection for the LGBT community in 1991. When they finally won a nondiscrimination ordinance for LGBT people in Jefferson County, Kentucky, in 1999, the band reunited to help celebrate, singing Carol Kraemer's lyrics, "All we want is just fairness, fairness now."[1]

Yer Girlfriend recorded three albums: *We Won't Be Silent!* (1989, Esther Records), *L-Word Spoken Here* (1992, Esther Records), and *Not Afraid to Love* (1995, Esther Records). Founding members Laura Shine (vocals, songwriting) and Carol Kraemer (vocals, guitar, main songwriter) started playing together as CLD Club in 1988. They were joined that summer by Kathy Weisbach (banjo, bass), in November by Phyllis Free (drums), and in spring 1989 by Patty O. Veranda (Martha Barnette, flute, keyboard). This group of

---

1 For more on the Fairness Campaign, see Carla F. Wallace, "The Fairness Campaign: Winning LGBTQ Rights By Building an Antiracist Majority," *Sinister Wisdom* 93 (Summer 2014): 84–87. Wallace describes the band as "the soundtrack for a struggle that captured the hearts and minds of an entire community" (p. 85).

five made the first two albums and is the group that plays reunion concerts. Patty O. Veranda and Kathy Weisbach left the band in 1993, and new members joined, including Liz Welsh (vocals, bass, acoustic, and electric guitar), Cindy Campbell (keyboard, flute), and Lisa Cates (percussion, drums, vocal). These three joined Laura, Carol, and Phyllis on the third album, *Not Afraid to Love*.

Carol and Laura started playing music together in 1988, while Carol was director of a senior center in Louisville. From 1996 to 2004, Carol was Organizational Manager of Louisville's LGBTQ rights organization, the Fairness Campaign. She currently directs a scholarship fund for student activists, the Davis–Putter Fund (www.davisputter.org). In 1992, Laura debuted a women's music program, *WomenWaves*, on WFPL 89.3 FM, a public radio affiliate in Louisville. She had started with WFPL 89.3, and then when the stations switched formats, she went to WFPK 91.9, and has been with this sister station (now all music) since 1996 in various capacities ever since, currently as assistant program director, and host of the afternoon drive time show and of their live music show, *Live Lunch*.

Yer Girlfriend played many women's music festivals, including the Southern Women's Music & Comedy Festival in north Georgia (1989 and 1990), all six Rhythm Fests (in Georgia, North Carolina, and South Carolina, 1990–95), the National Women's Music Festival in Bloomington, IN (1991 and 1993), and several other smaller festivals in the region. They were especially popular as a dance band and sometimes as unpaid performers at benefit concerts.

They loved to play at what they termed "mini-festivals" at "Connie's Cabin," a rural venue in southern Indiana, owned by their friend Connie Poole, and the site of many long-running lesbian parties. It was at Connie's Cabin that it all began. Or as Laura and Carol describe it:

> So we're out at the cabin. It's fall, and it's cold, and we're
> out on the screened porch. Phyllis sets up her drums, and

Kathy has her bass, and we just start playing. We did Maxine Feldman's "Amazon," did this really eerie, crazy version of it. And something magic happened right then, and we knew it. It felt great! That's really when Yer Girlfriend started to come together. We could see where the future could go.[2]

The community helped Yer Girlfriend throw a huge fundraiser out at the Cabin, a mini-music festival. Everybody played music all day long and way into the night. There was a stage built for them, a sort of treehouse stage. With this, and additional support from members of the local community, Yer Girlfriend raised enough funds to record their first album, *We Won't Be Silent*, recorded at Studio 2002 in New Albany, IN.

Yer Girlfriend became a popular dance band and performed at numerous benefits. Laura describes how that worked:

We all had such a strong passion for playing music. For Carol in particular it was an outlet for her politics, a creative outlet to be political. It was a way to fuse creativity with politics. We got the benefits of that because Carol was such a strong songwriter. We would all pitch in a little bit. She'd bring songs to the band and we'd discuss them and talk about arrangement. Maybe Martha might talk about it with Carol on a more intellectual level. Then we would get a song and present it to the community, and for the community it would become an anthem, or something that was really, really meaningful. We're all in this struggle together. That's how Yer Girlfriend kind of became a mouthpiece for the community.

And it didn't just have major political ramifications. It had major *personal* ramifications. We used to get told over and over again, "I'm so glad I had your tape with me. I had to drive all the way home to (say) Birmingham, and I couldn't

---

2 From Rose Norman's interviews with Carol Kraemer and Laura Shine, both Louisville natives, Louisville, KY, July 30, 2015. All quotations are from these interviews, unless otherwise noted.

be myself with my family, and that was really stressful. Your tape is what got me there and got me back. I listened to it over and over again." We heard those kinds of stories all the time. Our music was affirming to people's relationships, to their loves, to their political beliefs, to stay strong in a very homophobic world, and that's what Yer Girlfriend was there for.

That's what we did. When we played, we created community. We created a safe place for people to come and be themselves, and have fun, and dance, and love and laugh and be silly. All those things. Our band always felt to me more like an act of social work rather than going out there to get a bunch of praise. It was like a service to the community—a sermon for the community. It was a place to gather. It had a kind of church feel to it though there was nothing religious about it. Just religious in practice.

It was really a special, special thing. We felt owned by the community. The community knew we were their band, and they would follow us everywhere, even to the March on Washington, or New York, or South Carolina—just about everywhere we played. Any festival we played, at least somebody came, but usually an entourage would come to support us and be a part of that vibe.

And in turn, the women in Yer Girlfriend were personally affected by the music they wrote and performed:

Carol: We came up against our own internalized homophobia, when we did road trips. We'd be in small towns, and it didn't even matter if we were in the South (and we were mostly in the Southeast), but we went to Milwaukee and Chicago. I had huge internalized homophobia and fear, like will we get kicked out of this Cracker Barrel because people are being too out? Do we look too dykey? For me, it was part of my own personal process of figuring that out. I had a lot of fear in those moments of thinking whether it would be OK for the five, six, seven or eight of us fairly dykey looking women to go in.

Laura: Here you are writing these out and proud songs, and then inside you are absolutely torn apart. It was to overcome your own prejudices and fears.

Carol was even led to come out to her parents, after she had been in Yer Girlfriend for two years, because a local newspaper was reviewing their first album, *We Won't Be Silent.*

Yer Girlfriend's enormous role in reporting and reforming the view of lesbians in the South is a cultural accomplishment to be proud of. And they did this by living up to the key statement of their first album, "We won't be silent, we won't back down." And they did not.

Photo by Debra Clem

YER GIRLFRIEN

Publicity photo for first album, *We Won't Be Silent!* (1989), taken at Connie's Cabin (l to r): Laura Shine, Carol Kraemer, Kathy Weisbach, Phyllis Free, Patty O. Veranda.

TAKE BACK OUR LIVES[1]

Carol J. Kraemer

Carrie was only five years old when she learned how to hate herself
She had grown to love and trust the man that took her mother's hand
When one afternoon while Mom was away, he scarred her for life
In her room in the middle of the day.

Amy learned that she had no choice at 16 on her very first date
With the friend of a friend a very nice boy from a very nice family
He was out to prove he was a man, didn't care what she had to say
In the park in the middle of the day

Chorus: It's not just the night we must take back
We must reclaim our very lives
Women rise and demand the day
Rise up and take back our lives

Sara was a newlywed when she found how little she was worth
The man she thought she knew and loved laid claim to her body and soul
But even though she denied and screamed and cried, he forced his way
In her home in the middle of the day

It's not just the night we must take back
We must reclaim our very lives
Women rise and demand the day
Rise up and take back our lives

And now we sit in a circle, holding each other close
Remembering our darkened pasts
Joining hands for a future with a choice

1 © 1990 by Carol Kraemer. Four other songs by Carol Kraemer are online at http://www.sinisterwisdom.org/YerGirlfriend (with Kraemer's permission).

Joining hearts for a future with a voice
When will we have a choice?
When will we have a voice?

It's not just the night we must take back
We must reclaim our very lives
Women rise and demand the day
Rise up and take back our lives

REEL WORLD STRING BAND

Sue Massek

Reel World String Band came together for the first time in 1977 to perform for a celebration in honor of the International Women's Year at the University of Kentucky. For thirty-eight years we have followed the path pioneered by women like Florence Reece and Sarah Ogan Gunning, activist singer/songwriters from the coal fields of eastern Kentucky during the "Bloody Harlan" era in the 1930s. Their songs were a mainstay for many social justice movements and sung by folk icons Woody Guthrie and Pete Seeger. We were also heavily influenced by Hazel Dickens and Alice Gerrard, the first women's duo to make it in the mainstream of bluegrass music. With the exception of Alice, all of these women mentored us through the work of the Highlander Center in New Market, TN. Alice, who is the only one still living, continues to perform and mentor future generations of folk musicians. We were also deeply inspired by old-time Kentucky musicians such as Lily May Ledford, Jean Ritchie, and Blanche Coldiron, who opened opportunities for women to perform Appalachian music in public. We were honored to be included in *Kentucky Women: Two Centuries of Indomitable Spirit and Vision*, by Eugenia K. Potter (1997).

Original band members were Bev Futrell (guitar, mandolin, and harmonica), Sue Massek (banjo and guitar), Karen Jones (fiddle, guitar, and mandolin), Sharon Ruble (bass), and Belle Jackson (guitar). Elise Melrood (piano) joined Reel World in 1995, though she appeared on several of our recordings prior to joining the band. We all came from different musical and cultural backgrounds. Sharon and Belle were both native Kentuckians whose families were steeped in traditional Kentucky music. Bev grew up in central Texas listening to Western Swing. Karen, who was classically trained, grew up in Wisconsin and learned to play traditional Appalachian music from noted old-time fiddler, Guy

Blakeman. I grew up in Kansas in a family who regularly played traditional music from Appalachia at family gatherings. Elise, also from Wisconsin, is primarily a jazz pianist. All of these varied streams of music converged to create our "feminist hillbilly" niche.

We were one of the very first all-lesbian string bands and deeply involved with the political and cultural aspects of the GLBT movement. We, however, understood the intersectional nature of all oppressions and bigotry and consequently performed at venues and benefits for a wide variety of social justice and environmental issues. I believe our longevity is partially a result of our social justice focus. It has given the music we make together a purpose, and that makes it bigger than any one of us. We were honored to receive the Kentucky Center for Community and Justice Lauren K. Weinberg Humanitarian Award, on October 14, 2011.

In the early years we were nurtured by AmberMoon, a women's production company in Lexington, KY, and mentored by the Highlander Center in New Market, TN, an adult education and research center that trains grassroots organizers who are working on social justice issues. They taught us the power of the arts to create progressive social change and gave us an understanding of the interconnectedness of all the issues. Gatherings organized by Guy and Candie Carawan brought together artists and activists as varied as Rosa Parks and Nimrod Workman.

Many of the traditional string band songs were racist or sexist and sometimes both. So we evolved through the years from doing predominantly traditional fiddle tunes to doing songs Bev and I had written or songs written by folks like Hazel Dickens, Si Khan, and other socially conscious songwriters.

At first we played at lot of bluegrass festivals, but it wasn't a comfortable fit. Bluegrass fans expected a different sound and energy level than old-time music, and they wanted the familiar. We ultimately backed off bluegrass festivals and stuck to old-time, folk, and women's festivals.

We played most of the larger regional and national women's festivals in the eastern half of the nation, Michigan Womyn's Music Festival, the National Women's Music Festival, Southern Women's Music & Comedy Festival, Rhythm Fest, and Sisterfire. It was always a thrill to be playing for all those women, and the square dances were a sight to behold.

Though we were all lesbians and identified with the political and social aspects of the gay and lesbian movement, we never considered that to be the most important issue to support. How open we were at various venues depended on how safe it felt; we only came out at those venues that showed support for gay, lesbian, and feminist issues.

When Reel World first began, just being an "all-women band" was a feminist statement. Our choice of material was driven by the injustices most on our mind at the time, along with enough comic relief and old fiddle tunes to give the audience a break from the politics. If we couldn't find a song already written that was appropriate, we'd try to write one. We worked by consensus, each of us having veto powers (rarely used), so unless everyone agreed the song seemed like a good fit for us, we wouldn't do it.

We have been deeply connected to several state and regional nonprofit organizations working on peace, justice, and environmental issues. We've become the "house band" for the Cumberland Chapter of the Sierra Club, and we've played innumerable benefits for Kentuckians for the Commonwealth, the Appalachian Women's Alliance, and the New Opportunities for Women School. We've been awarded various Kentucky Foundation for Women Grants through the years and deeply appreciate their commitment to art for social change and the artists who are doing social justice work.

The band provided songs for soundtracks of various independent movies: *The Southern Sex, You Got to Move, From Calumet to Kalamazoo,* and *Shelter.* Many of our songs have been published in *Sing Out*, *Southern Exposure*, and *Speaking for Ourselves*.

We have made nine different recordings, beginning with three vinyl recordings—*Reel World String Band*, *Long Way to Harlan*, and *In Good Time*—followed by CD recordings: *Appalachian Wind*, *Whatnots*, *The Coast Is Clear*, *Live Music*, and *Mountain Songs: Reflections*, a CD compilation of the vinyl years, 1981–84. We also appeared on Joyce Brookshire's CD, *Cabbagetown Ballad*, a CD of women's coal mining songs, *They'll Never Keep Us Down*, and a *Sisterfire* Anthology.

Photo courtesy of Sue Massek

Reel World String Band circa 1980. Sharon Ruble on bass, Karen Jones in back with fiddle, Bev Futrell with mandolin, Bell Jackson in back with guitar, and Sue Massek with banjo.

WOMEN MAKE MUSIC: THE "LONG CIVIL RIGHTS" MOVEMENT, LADYSLIPPER MUSIC, AND DURHAM'S LESBIAN FEMINIST COMMUNITY, 1976–86

Molly Helen Chadbourne

The story of Ladyslipper Music in Durham, NC, provides a cross-section of how lesbian culture and lesbian-feminist activism intersected. Beth York excerpted Molly Helen Chadbourne's undergraduate honors thesis (UNC-Chapel Hill, 2007) to create this essay, with editorial assistance from Laurie Fuchs. The work draws on Chadbourne's interviews with Joanne Abel, Laurie Fuchs, Mandy Carter, Kathy Rudy, and Barb Smalley. Joanne Abel and Mandy Carter still serve on the Ladyslipper board.[1] Long-time staff members Liz Snow and Sue (Subie) Brown are shown in illustrations but were no longer working at Ladyslipper nor living in Durham in 2007, when Chadbourne conducted these interviews. Ladyslipper Music still exists as a music label and an online catalogue: https://www.ladyslipper.org

Introduction

In early May of 1986, Mab Segrest, along with members of the Durham Pride Committee and Triangle Area Lesbian-Feminists (TALF) of Durham, NC, drafted an antidiscriminatory proclamation signed by the mayor, calling on Durham to protect all its citizens from discrimination regardless of "affectional orientation" and declaring June 22–29 "Gay and Lesbian Pride Week." Joanne Abel and Nancy Blood, two lesbian librarians, made a display case of gay and lesbian literature and culture at Durham's public library,

---

1 These interviews are archived separately from the more recent interviews for the Southern Lesbian Feminist Activist Herstory Project, but are in the Sallie Bingham Center for Women's History and Culture at Duke University.

to go along with the celebration. Joanne had played a key role in the establishment of Ladyslipper Music. Vitriolic challenges to the proclamation, library exhibit, and Pride Week were immediate. Local Christian fundamentalists formed Citizens for Traditional Moral Government and started a petition to recall the mayor. Progressive citizens countered with the formation of Citizens for Responsible Leadership and organized against the recall. The Pride controversy dominated local newspapers between June and August, 1986. The successful struggle of Durham's politicized lesbians and gay men achieved unprecedented attention for Durham's gay and lesbian citizens, many of whom remember it as one of the most important events in Durham's history.[2] On June 29, 1986, nearly one thousand gay and straight citizens marched through the streets of Durham celebrating gay and lesbian visibility. A local bookstore closed, and its staff left a sign on the door that said "We're at the march. You should be, too."[3]

This event is indirectly part of the history of Ladyslipper Music, the Durham-based organization that has defined, publicized, and distributed women's music since 1976. Some Ladyslipper employees individually participated in the march. The very decision to have a march that included a pro-lesbian/gay mayoral proclamation resulted in large part from what was in 1986 more than ten years of building a lesbian-feminist community in Durham. TALF and Ladyslipper drew lesbian-feminists to Durham and connected Durham's lesbian-feminists to communities elsewhere. Ladyslipper produced concerts that created venues where lesbian and heterosexual feminists could

---

2   Mandy Carter, personal interview, September 7, 2007; Joanne Abel, personal interview, April 3, 2007. All quotations are to these interviews unless otherwise noted. The accomplishments of the 1986 Pride March are discussed twenty years later by Durham citizens in the *Independent Weekly's* September 27, 2006 "Pink Triangle" Special Issue. Jim Baxter, "Remembering the First PrideFest," *Pink Triangle*, ed. Lisa Song, special issue of *The Independent Weekly*, 7 (September 27, 2006).

3   Mandy Carter, personal interview, September 7, 2007.

meet. As distributors and producers of what came to be known as "women's music," Ladyslipper Music contributed to feminist and lesbian consciousness-raising and participated in the creation of a national feminist culture ("by, for, and about women," accurately portraying women's lives) that played an essential role in the second wave of the women's movement in the United States.

Courtesy of Laurie Fuchs

LADYSLIPPER CATALOG *and resource guide*

1989

RECORDS
TAPES
CD's
VIDEOS

by women

Ladyslipper catalog for 1989 with cover art by Sudie Rakusin. This was the first year to feature work by the local North Carolina lesbian feminist visual artist extraordinaire Sudie Rakusin, who donated use of her beautiful artwork for the catalog covers for many years.

In Durham, Ladyslipper constructed, produced, and distributed lesbian-feminist culture that appealed to feminists regardless of their sexual orientation. Ladyslipper also created economic and social opportunities for women. In the process, they confronted and attempted to resolve contradictions between capitalist business practices and feminist emphasis on social and economic justice. Ladyslipper also connected lesbian-feminists to other progressive activist organizations and, when artists requested, provided women-only venues for their events.

The women of Ladyslipper Music were among the mass of individuals who came together and formed coalitions and ways of life on the heels of the civil rights movement in the South. The triumphs of these women belong to a narrative of the "long civil rights movement," a term used by Jacquelyn Hall to suggest that it is "precisely the point when most Americans believe the [civil rights] movement ended, in the mid-1960's, that the South embarked on decades of change rivaling in scope and impact the events of the tumultuous 1950's and 1960's."[4]

Women's Music and Lesbian-Feminist Politics

Music has historically played an important role in social movements. The mobilization of the lesbian-feminist movement in the 1970s was directly connected to women's music.[5] The impact of women's music on Laurie Fuchs influenced her desire to make such music available to women across the country. Since the early 1970s, lesbian-feminists like Laurie played key roles in the establishment of a women's music movement, creating art

---

4 Southern Oral History Program, University of North Carolina, Chapel Hill.

5 Ron Eyerman and Andrew Jamison explain music's relationship to social movements as "the mobilization of tradition," arguing that "musical and other kinds of cultural traditions are made and remade, and after the movements fade away as political forces, the music remains as a memory and as a potential way to inspire new waves of mobilization." See their *Music and Social Movements: Mobilizing Traditions in the Twentieth Century* (Cambridge: Cambridge University Press, 1998), p. 1.

forms through which politics and visibility could be expressed. Many women across the United States found support for coming out as lesbians and feminists through the songs of lesbian artists. Women's music is often understood as "lesbian music" because the women's culture that evolved in the early businesses and organizations to support the growing women's music industry was founded by lesbians. Women's music in the 1970s was an inclusive term that feminists could call their own.

In July 1976, Laurie Fuchs and her sister took advantage of the growing women's cultural network and attended the third annual National Women's Music Festival in Champaign, IL. There they heard Malvina Reynolds talk about the importance of having women produce and distribute their own music. Malvina's message was "Don't trust the boys, do it yourself." The early women's music scene was full of energy and excitement, making Laurie's idea of distributing music feasible. Kathy Tomyris had already begun distributing Olivia Records in Durham. When Laurie returned home, she shared her idea with Joanne Abel, and they decided to distribute a wider variety of music by feminist artists, especially those appearing in women's music festivals and local events.

Laurie's idea of distributing music became a reality in the fall of 1976 when she started *Creatrix*, a women's craft collective mail-order catalog. The music she loved took up the back four pages. Although Laurie intended to focus on the crafts aspect of *Creatrix*, orders began coming in for music. The enterprise expanded in 1977 when Laurie placed a flyer for Ladyslipper in *Lesbian Connection*, a Michigan-based nationally distributed newsletter of lesbian culture started in 1974. Because *Lesbian Connection* already had an established readership, the flyer generated new orders. Partnering with Kathy Tomyris, the Durham distributor for Olivia Records, enabled both enterprises to launch the catalog at the second Michigan Womyn's Music Festival in August 1977. The festival was an opportunity for Ladyslipper to expand. The festival had no vendor tables or tents. Laurie and Kathy passed out 1500 catalogues, securing them underneath attendees' windshield wipers.

After Michigan, women's bookstores began to request orders from Ladyslipper, so Laurie and Kathy began distributing wholesale to women's bookstores nationally. Joanne recalled:

> This hadn't been part of their original plan—there was no plan—but requests kept coming in, and they realized this could be a big part of the mission. In fact, in the early years, wholesale was much more important than retail as a method of making many recordings more widely available.

Ladyslipper's success distributing wholesale forced Laurie and Kathy to contemplate the potential of selling items representing "women's culture." The idea of taking money for profit from other feminists by selling items that communicated a feminist vision seemed to contradict feminist goals. In the 1978 catalogue, Kathy addressed this problem:

> There is a contradiction between selling plasticized music for a living, while at the same time encouraging our consumers to become feminists and revolutionaries. We want all women to work to change the patriarchal/capitalist system that oppresses us all (and out of which the very concept of profit comes). We want you to buy our records so that (or because) you will come to love and respect women as much as we do; enough to make the changes that will put us and all other profit-oriented businesses out of business, You won't hear that message directly in much of the music we offer. Its message is rather that women are strong, intelligent, talented, and capable. From that, it is up to you to join with women organizing and struggling to end oppression. We encourage you to support feminist organizations and businesses working for change.[6]

---

6 *Ladyslipper Catalogue*, Spring, 1978.

Laurie Fuchs working the Ladyslipper booth at Sisterfire in 1983.

Over the next five years, Ladyslipper changed locations, became neighbors with a cluster of other progressive organizations, and reorganized as a nonprofit educational organization. They were able to employ more women, both lesbian and straight. The 1980s brought about considerable change in Ladyslipper's role within the local lesbian-feminist community. The "Slippers" continued to produce concerts and made critical connections with other Durham activists. The difficult task of organizing concerts would not have been possible without support of the local community. The 1985 catalog acknowledges the important contributions of volunteers and friends of Ladyslipper: "Women from our communities lend their hands as volunteers for special projects, and friends from around the country assist . . . by giving loans, gifts, information, so this work is genuinely the fruit of many."[7]

7 *Ladyslipper Catalogue & Resource Guide: Records & Tapes by Women,* 1985: 2.

Photo by Gayle Scott

Ladyslipper's founder Laurie Fuchs (right) with Liz Snow (left). Liz worked full-time at Ladyslipper 1978–88 and was instrumental in reorganization as a nonprofit. Here they are selling records at the Ladyslipper booth, Michigan Womyn's Music Festival, circa the early 1980s.

Ladyslipper's neighbors adjacent to their new office space at 602 West Chapel Hill Street included both the Institute for Southern Studies, a progressive organization that published *Southern Exposure Magazine*,[8] and the War Resisters League

---

8   The Institute for Southern Studies is still based in Durham and publishes a magazine called *Facing South*, https://www.facingsouth.org/. Currently, a magazine called *Southern Exposure* is published out of Atlanta but is not focused on social justice issues.

(WRL).[9] Mandy Carter, an employee of the WRL, began working for Ladyslipper during this time. Initially, Mandy was not sure what to expect as a Black lesbian moving to the South from San Francisco. "When I was moving here, someone said, 'Where are you going to be moving to, Mandy?' I said, 'North Carolina.' The reaction was, 'Don't they still lynch people out there?' And I had this same image." But when she moved to Durham, she realized the extent of the lesbian-feminist community. "San Francisco was very male-dominated. I came to Durham, and lesbians were not quite running everything, but it seemed very close to it." Mandy believed that the lesbian feminist community grew and was so strong in Durham because of the strong Black community already present. For her "it was nice to be just one of many in a community with a long legacy of Blackness." Kathy Rudy, who also worked at Ladyslipper, recognized that the lesbian-feminist community was part of an ongoing struggle for justice in the South.

From the1980s and into the 1990s, Ladyslipper continued to grow and change. In 1982, Ladyslipper began producing artists on its own label, Ladyslipper Records. The first album studio-produced by Ladyslipper in 1984 was Kay Gardner's *A Rainbow Path*, which sold over ten thousand copies in six months. That success was followed with albums by Beth York (*Transformations*, 1985), Casselberry-DuPree (*Hot Corn in the Fire*, 1994), Nuru (*Drum Call*, 1994), and Ubaka Hill (*ShapeShifters*, 1995), and many others. The year 1986 was also important for the Durham community. Ladyslipper celebrated its tenth anniversary while progressive citizens of Durham celebrated the triumph of staging a successful Pride March and defeating an attempted mayoral recall. Ladyslipper became one of the most comprehensive databases of women's music in the world while still maintaining its commitment to the local community. In 1988 the "Slippers" created a listening

---

9 The War Resisters League has continuously been a leading voice in antiwar efforts since its founding in 1923. For more history on the WRL, see http://www. warresisters.org/.

room at their offices so students and local customers could relax and hear new women's music.

The spring 1981 concert season was very ambitious!

But by the early 1990s, conflicts related to economic issues returned to haunt Ladyslipper. They stopped producing frequent concerts when production costs became prohibitive. As Laurie Fuchs explained:

In the beginning they were small enough that if you lost a hundred dollars, you took it out of your own pocket. But our pockets weren't that deep, and a hundred dollars would have been a big loss to us then. As the stakes got bigger, and the guarantees got bigger, you could lose a thousand dollars in an evening.[10]

It is ironic that the success of women's music began the change in the music industry as a whole. As women's music artists became more mainstream, customers had more options and less need to support women's music distribution outlets. Borders and online companies like Amazon threatened the thriving independent music distribution networks and bookstores that supported women's culture, and the organizations stopped growing. Laurie explained that for a number of years, the organization grew at a comparable rate to the growth of women's bookstores. When

---

10 Laurie Fuchs, personal interview, August 3, 2007. All quotations are to this interview unless otherwise noted.

women's bookstores began to close, Ladyslipper lost many significant outlets for its recordings. In 1996, the Ladyslipper catalog expanded into an online resource: www.ladyslipper.org.

Photo courtesy of Laurie Fuchs

Ladyslipper staff in 1981. Top: Liz Snow and Laurie Fuchs. Bottom: Pat Wilkerson and Sue (Subie) Brown. Pat was a work-study employee in 1981. Subie worked there 1980–87.

But perhaps it is not that Ladyslipper could no longer compete with the megastores. Perhaps it is that Ladyslipper was a catalyst for change within the mainstream. Perhaps Ladyslipper opened the door for lesbian artists and musicians to enter into the mainstream and for recording companies to become more inclusive. Mandy Carter is positive about Ladyslipper's history:

Sometimes when something goes away it is not necessarily a bad thing. I think sometimes things go away because whatever particular role that it had to play in that moment of time was just so spectacular. If things move on and transform, it's not a sad thing. It's great if you had a role to play. That is fantastic. Make sure that people don't forget it.[11]

The work of establishing lesbian-feminist women's culture, demonstrated by Ladyslipper Music, altered the political landscape. Without this work, many feminist artists would not have gained visibility. By helping to establish a women's culture, both locally and nationally, Ladyslipper participated in feminist consciousness-raising. The network not only helped women come out as lesbians but also enabled women to start organizations to support themselves and form communities. The safety of place and creation of the genre of women's music enriched and sustained the activists of the second wave of feminism in the United States.

Ladyslipper's story contradicts narratives of waning political activity in the post-1960s South. The cultural feminist movement of the 1970s and 1980s was a time of political growth and activism. Women came out and established themselves as independent feminists, lesbians, and heterosexuals alike. Women created an arts network out of which they could support themselves and each other economically. The civil rights movement was taken up and transformed into new forms. To appreciate this crucial element of Southern history, women's history, and gay and lesbian history is to better understand our past and the shoulders upon which we stand. The importance of these stories is articulated perfectly by one of Durham's best-known lesbian feminists, Mab Segrest: "The future is nothing if not what we love in the past, set free."[12]

---

11 Mandy Carter, personal interview, September 7, 2007.

12 This is the closing line of "Frances and Bell: 'When People Have to Choose . . .'" in Segrest's *My Mama's Dead Squirrel: Lesbian Essays on Southern Culture* (Ithaca, NY: Firebrand Books), p. 176.

LESBIAN MUSIC PRODUCERS: "LEAPIN' LESBIANS"

Woody Blue and Beth York

A single note, rising in the hushed room, commands attention. We are stilled, eyes and ears focused on the brightly lit stage. The notes build into chords, then a riff, then the beginnings of a familiar song. It's Marathon, it's Margie Adam, it's Ferron, it's Teresa Trull, it's Disappear Fear, it's the Reel World String Band, it's a womyn's music concert, music by womyn, for womyn. The audience leans in to listen to the words, entrapped and enthralled. An American Sign Language (ASL) signer sways and signs to deaf womyn in the front row.

Some womyn silently mouth the words; some bob their heads. It is hard to sit still. A couple leave their chairs, walk to the side aisle. Standing in the shadows, they rock right to left. Arms swing back and forth to the music. More womyn join them and begin to dance. Soon the aisles are filled with dancers. Those still sitting, sway in their seats. The music sweeps through the room. No one holds back. The musicians pump it out, let loose, working their voices, diving into their instruments, meeting the energy created by the womyn in the audience.

Chairs are pushed back, womyn are on their feet, clapping, cheering. It's a regular insurrection. They don't call it a womyn's movement for nothing.

At a time when homosexuality was looked at as a mental disease, when womyn couldn't get credit cards, before womyn's studies programs spread, lesbians around the South and around the country took on the task of building a lesbian music network. Inspired by the Michigan Womyn's Music Festival, Southern lesbians returned home and formed collectives to actualize a vision of lesbian culture. The vision encompassed bringing lesbians and other womyn together to build nonhierarchical organizations where every womon found her power, devoid of patriarchal interference. The Voting Rights Act in 1965 had brought racial issues to the forefront, and white and Black lesbian feminists worked to tear down the walls that separated them.

Radical lesbian feminists accepted the challenge, individually and collectively, to bring lesbian culture to Southern cities, towns, and rural areas. They inspired each other to find, take, and use their power to generate a female-centric culture. In the Southern United States, where the good old boys prided themselves on keeping their women under control, lesbians rolled up their sleeves and went to work.

As early as 1976, Ceci Mitchell, Margo George, and Isabel Bagshaw, fresh from the first Michigan Womyn's Music Festival, came back to Atlanta, determined to bring lesbian musicians and performers home to their Southern sisters. Ten womyn "banded together, calling themselves Lucina's Music, committed to the production and propagation of Women's Music and Culture."[1]

The Lucina's Music collective based itself on feminist principles of shared leadership, irrespective of differences in class and race. Feminist ethics were evident in consensus decision-making and the equal division of labor. Even though the Americans with Disabilities Act was not passed until 1990, Lucina's Music and other producers throughout the South provided ASL signing and front row seating for deaf womyn, as well as ramps for concert-goers with physical challenges. They offered sliding scale ticket prices and work exchange opportunities for low-income women. They provided free childcare.

---

1 The Exegesis of Lucina's Music, n.d., Box 23, ALFA Archives, Sallie Bingham Center for Women's History and Culture in the Rubenstein Rare Book & Manuscript Library at Duke University. Beth York did a group interview with former Lucina's Music and Orchid members: Maria Dolan, Chris Carroll, Liz Hill, Jo Hamby, and Rebeca [sic] Quintana. The interview was conducted on September 26, 2010, at the home of Chris Carroll and Maria Dolan, Atlanta, GA. She interviewed two additional founders, Judy Aehle and Ceci Mitchell, on July 18 and July 20, 2011. All quotations are from these interviews.

Record sales were handled by individual artists and through the Women's Independent Label Distribution (WILD) network (WILD) that included Ladyslipper, Redwood, and Olivia Records. Lucina's first production was Andrea Weltman and Britches, a blues and rock band who had worked with West Coast artists. "Big hair, very tall," Chris Carroll remembers.

Courtesy of Rubenstein Rare Book & Manuscript Library, Duke University. Used with permission of Orchid Productions

ORCHID PRODUCTIONS, INC.
Post Office Box 5585 • Atlanta, Georgia 30307

Orchid Productions logo.

Chris was already hosting a radio show on Atlanta's WRFG called "Still Ain't Satisfied." She was also hosting listening parties to introduce women's music to Atlanta lesbians. Usually Lucina's produced seven or eight events over a twelve-month period. That included concerts in large venues like the World Congress Center with nationally known artists like Meg Christian, Holly Near, and Cris Williamson, as well as local benefit concerts at the Little Five Points Pub for the Atlanta Council on Battered Women, Karuna Counseling, and the Atlanta Lesbian Feminist Alliance (ALFA). Lucina's lasted until 1981, succeeded by Orchid Productions, who continued to produce artists from the women's music circuit until 1987. A concert by Atlanta artist Beth York and her chamber ensemble was the last concert Orchid produced.

Further north, Mother's Brew, a lesbian bar in Louisville, KY (1975–79) took on the task in a different way. They had a house band, River City Wimmin, but also regularly brought in national talent. Manager Jade River describes how that worked:

> [We would] have somebody about twice a month from the women's music industry. We developed a network and took artists to other places where they could also do concerts. We'd drive them to Cincinnati, and someone there would drive them to Columbus [OH]. We formed a circuit of women's music artists. They'd either go north or south, and frequently Mother's Brew would be their first stop.[2]

At the end of 1977, Ladyslipper Music in Durham, NC, began to produce women's music concerts, helping to create a more cohesive and recognizable sense of community for the women of Durham. Laurie Fuchs remembered:

> Women's music concerts at the YMCA on Proctor Street were a crucial part of the feminist community. They became great social events. That was one of the reasons that the "women's music movement" was seen as an important center of culture.[3]

---

2   From a phone interview with Rose Norman, November 12, 2015.

3   Molly Helen Chadbourne, "Women Make Music: The 'Long Civil Rights' Movement, Ladyslipper Music, and Durham's Lesbian Feminist Community, 1975-1986," undergraduate Honors Thesis (UNC-Chapel Hill, 2007), p. 22. See also story this issue.

In the 1980s, Ladyslipper gained more of a reputation for their extensive catalog of womyn artists, concentrating on record promotion, sales, and distribution. To fill the gap, a group of lesbians formed Real Women Productions. Lucy Harris, Mandy Carter, Cheri Sistek, and Cris South produced concerts, dances, and "huge community events" from 1986 to 1990, including a Melissa Etheridge concert ("before she made it"), Holly Near, Kay Gardner, and the Indigo Girls. Blue Moon Productions followed in their footsteps, run by Lucy Harris and Babs Brown. Concerts were held in Durham and Chapel Hill in venues seating from 250 to 1200 attendees.[4] (That was "huge" back then.)

Nashville, Tennessee, is known as Music City, and womyn's music was a part of the scene in the late 1970s and 1980s. The Nashville Women's Coffeehouse opened in 1979, and womyn packed the house. Carole Powell and Joanna Morrison of Womankind Books produced concerts there from 1979 until 1983. Their productions were for women-only, but not exclusively lesbian. Dykes traveled for hours to see their favorite recording artists on stage—Meg Christian, Teresa Trull, Margie Adam, Cris Williamson, Linda Tillery—as well as local Nashville talent, who opened for them. Some local womyn musicians were out lesbians, but many had to be closeted. In the 1980s, being known as a lesbian in Nashville could mean the end of a career. Local performers were delighted to be able to play their music for an audience of dykes with whom they could be themselves, and to perform material they would not be able to play for mixed audiences. Dykes cheered for the likes of Willie Tyson, Sharon Riddell, Susan Abod, Dianne Davidson, Margie Plant, Annie McGowen, Beegee Adair, and lots of lesser-known but highly talented women. Through the efforts of Womankind's Carole Powell, working with Ginny Berson of Olivia Records, Nashville also hosted a gathering of feminist

---

4 From Rose Norman's interview with Lucy Harris and Babs Brown in Durham, NC, July 12, 2015.

womyn record distributors and concert producers, solidifying the Southern womyn's music scene.[5]

The women's music industry in the South continued to grow. In 1980, Ruth Segal and Sandy Malone went to see Alix Dobkin perform at Pagoda, a women's intentional community on Vilano Beach in St. Augustine, Florida. They ended up hanging out on the beach with her. When they said something about there being no women's music concerts in Gainesville, FL, Alix offered a deal. If they would agree to produce her the next year, she would teach them all she knew about producing a concert. They did, and Womyn Producing Womyn (WPW) was born.

Ruth and Sandy were committed to introducing other aspects of lesbian culture to Gainesville as well as producing lesbian music. Some of the "cross-cultural shape-shifters" included comedians Robin Tyler and Lea DeLaria, Z Budapest (a Wiccan lesbian), and JEB (a prominent lesbian photographer). Tee Corinne dazzled audiences with her erotic sexual art. WPW kept Gainesville rocking with music performed by the Berkeley Women's Music Collective, June Millington, and Ferron.[6]

About the same time in the deep south of Birmingham, AL, Lissa LeGrand and other local musicians and their friends created Magnolia Productions, a collective of about twenty lesbians. Some had moved to Birmingham from cities where there were blossoming lesbian cultural scenes that they wanted to bring to Birmingham. Lissa's band Marathon and others volunteered to perform concerts with local talent ("Magnolia Jams") to raise money to bring in nationally recognized musicians like Meg Christian, Willie Tyson, Cris Williamson, and Holly Near. Magnolia produced over twenty-five womyn's events in Birmingham between 1982 and 1987. Lissa recollects:

---

5 Nashville material is from Rose Norman's interview with Carole Powell, December 31, 2012.

6 Gainesville material is from Barbara Esrig's interview with Sandy Malone and Ruth Segal in Gainesville, FL, September 3, 2015.

It's interesting how many different factions of the lesbian community we reached. There was a fairly large element of lesbians we knew and recognized as family. Younger dykes were coming to our concerts. Older, [more closeted] folks would appear and cheer wildly for the artists and then disappear into the night, carefully and quietly.[7]

Photo courtesy of Lissa LeGrand

Birmingham's Marathon band playing day stage at MichFest 1986 (l-r): Shelley Chapman, keyboard; Lissa LeGrand, bass and vocals; Julie Trippe, sax, vocals, percussion; Carole Griffin, lead vocal, guitar; Regina Cates, drums, vocals; Josie Grab le, vocals, harmonica, lead, and rhythm guitar.

What these courageous Southern womyn's music producers held in common was a belief that music created lesbian community and made it stronger. They were in their twenties and thirties, and committed to promulgating feminist values through music. With few resources, little production experience, and no financial backing, they found a way to lay a solid networking foundation and build on it. Lesbian community, not profits, came first.

---

7   From Rose Norman's interview with Lissa LeGrand in Birmingham, AL, June 23, 2015.

Money was always scarce. Magnolia and Lucina's Music formed 501(c)(3) nonprofit corporations, which opened the door to apply for grants and to receive donations. Despite best efforts, collective members were rarely paid for their efforts. More often than not, says Orchid Production's Jo Hamby, "everything we made, we put back into the group." The effort to incorporate "cashless exchanges" to reduce overhead was an innovative strategy ("exchanging energies, doing childcare, tending concessions in exchange for admission") but could not meet the rising costs of publicity, artists' fees, and expectations for their care. As audiences grew, they tapped larger, more costly, mainstream spaces. Larger venues meant increased overhead and little to no profits.

The lack of funding couldn't stop the lesbian cultural tide sweeping the South. Collective members explored cheap, friendly venues like community centers, bars, sympathetic churches, and university spaces. They handled all aspects of production from marketing and promotion to running lights and sound systems, to hosting musicians, and cleaning up after the show. Serving refreshments helped the cash flow. At the end of a concert, audience members sometimes stayed to stack the chairs. In countless meetings, from Atlanta to Miami to Birmingham to Louisville to Durham, lesbian feminists hammered out policy regarding ticket prices, childcare issues, and ASL signing.

How do you advertise a women's music concert to attract lesbians? Passing the word around could be dangerous in the homophobic South, so they made announcements in meetings and at social events, and passed out flyers or posted them in bars, bookstores, and other places where lesbians congregated. In Gainesville, Ruth and Sandy snailmailed postcards to over a thousand women on their mailing list to announce their events.

Friendly dykes from the community often lent a hand. Rebeca [sic] Quintana of Orchid Productions remembers: "I did the layout for posters, press releases. I used my IBM Selectric II typewriter and the copy machine at Kinkos." Flyers explained that the music was "For women, By women, and About women." Women's events promoted sliding scale fees, ("more if you can, less if you can't") and work exchange ("Work half a day, pay half price; work a full day, free ticket"). Take note, we are talking about ticket prices at $3–$5.

On the nights of the concerts, the "glamour" was also shared. Selling tickets, stage management, being a member of the stage crew, and emceeing were thrilling positions to hold. Tough young butches adjusted microphones and lifted heavy amps as audience members wandered in. Lots of strutting, ogling, and flirting was going on before, during, and after the concerts.

From small beginnings in the 1970s, lesbian music producers opened up the South to lesbian performers from around the country. Recordings and distributorship played a vital role in knitting communities together and connecting to other regions of the country. Performers did their share to reach out and take advantage of the opportunities to expand their audiences. If a concert was held in a larger city that could afford the musician, a smaller town nearby could hold a small concert the next day for a smaller fee, sometimes with the sound equipment trailing along. It was common for musicians to sleep in local homes, eating whatever was served at the house, and for someone to host a community potluck. In this way, they built alliances, shared community and expenses.

"We gave them nothing other than whatever was in our kitchen," recalls Sandy Malone from Women Producing Women in Gainesville. "They got in whatever piece of shit automobile we owned, and we drove them to the Unitarian Church."

Building a womyn's music network in the South was a monumental task. None of the production groups we interviewed lasted into the new century. Though it was a highly rewarding endeavor, most of the dedicated women involved grew tired or burned out with the tremendous effort that producing concerts required.

But it was also deeply meaningful and moving. Rebeca Quintana reflects: "Being able to contribute to the community fed me, supported me. Through the arts is how you reach people. We weren't always appreciated. But at the concerts themselves . . . and the euphoria after the concert . . . I have fond memories of that high. It brought me closer to those people. When we see each other, we know what we did together." Sandy Malone remembers: "We made this happen, and it was so easy. It's not like it was a burden, or anybody was whining about how to lick the stamps. Standing in back of the room together, looking over the crowd with Ferron up there singing, knowing that we made this happen, it's just mind blowing." Jo Hamby takes a more emotional stance: "Live music touches me more than recorded music. The energy created puts a smile on people's faces. It brings us closer together, brings tears to our eyes."

The music drifts down from the stage, circling each womon before sailing out the door. It chases down the alley to the womyn holding hands. It rushes into the streets, the country roads, down the rivers. It finds the small sweet places in our womon souls bringing us up, pulling us together, giving us voice. It merges with the beaches, the bayous, the mountains, valleys, and hammocks. Here, in the South, womyn's music hovers in the sweet air as we breathe and remember. Yea, music! Yea lesbians! Womyn's music? Oh yeah, that's how we got this way. That's how we found each other.

ATLANTA FEMINIST WOMEN'S CHORUS
Charlene Ball

Origins

In the 1970s, lesbian and gay male choruses arose from burgeoning lesbian and gay cultures. So did feminist choruses, with both lesbian and straight women. Singing together in public as openly lesbian women or gay men became a way of coming out, proudly claiming public space, and creating community, while singing in feminist choruses asserted the power, creativity, and culture of women. The Atlanta Feminist Women's Chorus (AFWC), founded in 1981,[1] managed to combine both lesbian pride and feminism, creating a unique experience for the women who participated. This interview by Beth York with the AFWC's founding director Linda Vaughn and three former members of the chorus describes how the chorus got started and what it meant to some of the women who participated.[2]

Beth: Eleanor Smith's and Sharon Sanders' history of the chorus says that a few of you met at the ALFA House to sing and began to rehearse without a director. Then Linda Vaughn met Judy Aehle and asked if there was a women's chorus. Judy said, "No, but I know people who want to have one, and we need a director." Linda agreed to direct, and Judy spread the word and

---

1 A website for AFWC states that the group began in 1981: http://www.womenarts. org/network/profile_959.html. It was online and saying this as of 2013. The ALFA timeline gives the "first solo, full-length concert (at First Existentialist Church)" as of April 1983. There was a short concert at ALFA's tenth anniversary party in August 1982 (ALFA timeline). Legal documents say AFWC was incorporated in 1987. By 1988, the organizational structure had expanded to include an Assistant Director, President, Treasurer, Secretary, and committees: (1) publicity, (2) library, (3) social, (4) place, (5) membership, and (6) grants. The chorus also had an Auxiliary who ushered at concerts and sponsored fundraising events.

2 Beth York interviewed Judy Aehle, Linda Vaughn, Charlene Ball, and Shirley Chancey, on July 21, 2012, in Atlanta.

set up a meeting at ALFA House. Linda directed AFWC for twelve years, from 1981 to 1993.[3]

Linda: I had been in a women's chorus in Cincinnati. When I was transferred to Atlanta, I was looking for that woman energy. I felt a need [for] that connection.

Rehearsals, Reception, Repertoire, and Feminist Processes

Beth: Let's talk about early rehearsals in the tiny space at the ALFA House.

Linda: We would have sopranos in one room and altos in another. It quickly grew from twelve to twenty-five. At thirty, we moved to Eleanor Smith's house in Virginia Highlands.

Chancey: We rehearsed in different rooms. Linda would stand in the middle of the two rooms in the doorway [directing]. We rotated houses.

Beth: Then rehearsals moved to the First Existentialist Congregation of Atlanta.

Linda: A lot of the advertising was word of mouth. Charis Bookstore was important.

Beth: One report of the first concert says that . . . ten women wanted to join right away.

Chancey: When I saw the Chorus that first time, all of these people came barreling down the aisle at the ECong in their blue jeans, and I remember thinking, "Oh, I gotta be part of this." I was one of those ten women who came running up after the show.

Beth: You already had a sense of women-only space with women's music performers that Lucina's and Orchid had produced. By 1983, Orchid was folding. You come in the same year, build it into a grassroots experience for women to experience their own power and voices.

---

3 April 29, 1989, spring concert program, ALFA archives. AFWC archives are in the Special Collections and Archives, Georgia State University, Atlanta, but ALFA archives are in the Sallie Bingham Center for Women's History and Culture at Duke University, Durham, NC. The ALFA collection at Duke contains many AFWC documents.

Photo by Jan

Atlanta Feminist Women's Chorus. Director Linda Vaughn is far left, front row. (Charlene Ball Papers, manuscript # W102, Special Collections and Archives, Georgia State University, Atlanta.)

Chancey: You didn't have to audition. [Linda] molded us into something that people wanted to see and hear. They enjoyed the music, the performance, the show. But it was more than that. They wanted more of what they saw on stage—bonded, strong women.

Beth: You became role models. How did you decide to incorporate the word "feminist" into the name?

Linda: We voted. Some people would not identify with a [lesbian] group. They couldn't feel safe doing that. Not everyone was lesbian. Straight women joined.

Beth: So the term "feminist" was more inclusive. Looking at an early concert flyer (April 10, 1983), I see songs from Mozart, Cris Williamson, Holly Near. You didn't do *just* women's music. Choosing the music was a group process or . . . your decision?

Judy: Early on, Linda was it. [Linda] did a great job of balancing different kinds of music in the program. That's part of why people came. There was upbeat stuff, serious. No committee could have come up with that variety.

Linda: The music spoke to various audiences . . . [and] different strengths of the chorus members. We got people who had studied music [and] people who had never sung in a chorus before.

Charlene: Every concert had something that was zany and goofy, sexy, romantic, elevated, and spiritual.

Chancey: Later, a music selection committee was formed. Otherwise, every issue was done by consensus. [W]e kept a structure that allowed everyone a voice. [W]e would have serious disagreements, [but] everybody's desire was to make it work. It was precious, and we were going to savor every drop of it. We knew we were creating something unique.

Beth: It sounds like every woman felt heard in those meetings.

Chancey: [E]veryone was helping. "I'll get this Xeroxed." "We'll do this program." "I'll draw this."

Charlene: There was a lot of volunteering. Linda Rye did some of the artwork. I did press releases.

Chancey: We set our ticket prices, but if there were any organizations who let us know they were coming, like the battered women's shelter, we gave them tickets. If a woman wanted to come, but couldn't pay, they had to let us know. We helped chorus people who couldn't afford the uniforms.

Linda: Or someone who couldn't afford to travel.

Beth: By 1985, flyers advertising AFWC concerts [mentioned] sign language interpretation and wheelchair accessibility. You always had sign language interpretation.

Linda: Gail McKay. We auditioned signers.

Linda: We had . . . [members] in wheelchairs. We were part of the reason they built the ramp at the First Existentialist Congregation. I was approached by a woman who wanted to start an African American gay chorus in Atlanta. Our hopes were to combine the groups. [Over the years, eight African American women were chorus members.] We had Asian and . . . Native American women.

On Tour

Linda: The first trip out of Atlanta was the March on Washington in 1987. Robin Tyler [organizer of the Southern Women's Music & Comedy Festival] was handling the music for the March. She called and said she would like us to be the women's chorus there.

Linda: It was [our] first gay rights march. ABC News said 200,000 people marched that day, but I'd say it was a million.

Beth: Here's a letter to you from Jeff Cone:

I cannot tell you how proud it made us to hear . . . "The Atlanta Feminist Women's Chorus." . . . You looked great and sounded fantastic. . . . "Love is the Answer" had the crowd on its feet. . . . You were a major part of a weekend . . . that changed peoples' lives. You've secured a place for yourselves in lesbian and gay history. . . . [T]hank you for your excellent work. . . . !

Chancey: We referred to that concert as our "coming out." We saw the strength in community. Standing on that stage, looking across to the Washington Monument, seeing nothing but a sea of people.

Beth: [You took part in] a concert to celebrate Therese Edele's fortieth birthday in Cincinnati. [You traveled] to Denver for GALA [and] to Miami to sing with the Miami Gay Men's Chorus. [You became] a part of GALA [and networked] with choruses all over the country.[4] How were you invited to sing at Terese Edell's fortieth birthday?

Linda: Terese Edell . . . wanted us to come. When we got there, we were exhausted. The sound equipment died during the performance. [But] we were well received. We sang "Jubilant Song," a choral piece by Norman Dello Joio—exciting and far above our previous expertise.

---

4 GALA Choruses is an international alliance of 170 gay and lesbian men's, women's, and mixed choruses. GALA Choruses produce a choral festival every three years. www.galachoruses.org

Beth: [Other] "most memorable performances?"

Linda: [S]inging "Moon" in Miami [with the Miami Gay Men's Chorus]. People in the chorus were crying. I got that with "Jubilant Song," too.

Beth: In some of the classical and popular songs, you played with gender. When lesbians were singing, it gave the song a whole new meaning.

Photo by Jan

Atlanta Feminist Women's Chorus Director Linda Vaughn directing a rehearsal. (Charlene Ball Papers, manuscript # W102, Special Collections and Archives, Georgia State University, Atlanta.)

Linda: I would change lyrics occasionally, which was fun.

Charlene: There was a Brahms song, "I Send You Greetings," a love song to a woman by women, because we were singing it. When we were performing at Southside High School [Fall concert, 1990], two women sang love songs to each other; another woman sang a raunchy song.

Linda Vaughn Leaves

Beth: The April 10, 1993, program announced that Linda would be leaving the chorus as Director. Linda resigned after the spring concert of 1993. She had been director for twelve years.

Linda: 1993. I wasn't diagnosed yet, but I was sick. I thought I had done as much as I could. I announced it a year in advance. In retrospect, that was not a good thing to do. When it got to be a hundred voices, every week became a struggle.

Charlene: The times had changed. By then [the 1990s], there was no longer that sense of a united lesbian community.

Beth: We got older. Priorities changed. We were making life decisions. Were we going to have kids? Buy a house? We were thinking about establishing ourselves as adults.

Judy: We were having rehearsals sometimes two or three times a week.

Chancey: [G]oing to Florida, going to Cincinnati. [A] lot of people joined before or after those large events, like the March on Washington. We were a hundred-plus voices by then. Rehearsals were more complex. Our reputation . . . was building across the country. It's one thing to create a beautiful sound from thirty untrained singers, but to create that sound when you have over seventy-five untrained singers is quite another.

Beth: After Linda, Rev. Glenna Shepherd was Chorus Director (1992–93). Robert Glor was Interim Director and then Director from September 1994 to July 2000. Eileen Moreman was Director after Robert.[5]

Final Thoughts

Linda: There are lots of things I miss. The whole energy that is forever gone. You have people who never knew about or

---

5 Shepherd's dates are from her resume, http://www.decaturucc.org/about-us/leadership/rev-glenna-shepherd/employment-experience-and-education/. Robert Glor's dates are from Eileen Stone, President of the AFWC for several years.

experienced this movement. Now there are many outlets for music and many different role models.

Beth: How did being in the chorus change you?

Judy: It was a profound sense of community. The experience of singing regularly does something nice to you. I felt like I was a part of something bigger.

Chancey: I can remember walking up the ECong steps. I could feel the stress leaving my body.

Charlene: The Chorus helped [me] to be more in the world. It gave me creative inspiration.

Beth: I have a copy of the speech that Linda delivered to the chorus when she was leaving.

> *Dear Wonderful Chorus:*
>
> *As I think back on what being with this group has meant to me, some events come to mind....*
>
> *—Our first performance at the Acme Theatre with 100 screaming women in attendance*
>
> *—A jam packed E Cong with an enthusiastic rendition of Dolly [Parton's] "9-5."*
>
> *—The first Southern Women's Music Festival and a sizzling hot Mary, Carolyn, and 50-voice chorus rocking . . . the 1008+ mainstage crowd to "Sisters are Doin' it."*
>
> *—The return flight from the '87 March, when you could see on our faces the importance of what we had just accomplished—*
>
> *—A chorus member's joyous tears after her first concert—*
>
> *—Washington, '93 on the Kick Off Stage . . . —*
>
> *Your presence in this chorus has affected me in ways that can never be duplicated. I thank you for your hard work, great music, wonderful spirit, and endearing love. . . .[6]*

---

6 Excerpts from Letter to Chorus from Linda Vaughn (n.d.), AFWC Records, W-100, History of AFWC, 1988–91, Special Collections and Archives, Georgia State University, Atlanta.

CRESCENDO, THE OLDEST LESBIAN CHORUS STILL SINGING IN THE SOUTHEAST

Sage Morse

Crescendo was founded in August 1991 as the Tampa Bay Gay Women's Chorus, and made its debut at the Tampa Bay Gay Men's Chorus' holiday concert that year. The driving idea behind its founding was to co-host GALA (Gay and Lesbian Association of Choruses) in 1996. It was soon clear that there was a need for a lesbian chorus in the area, and in 1992 it became Crescendo: The Tampa Bay Womyn's Chorus. The mission statement has been modified over the years, but it states: "Founded on lesbian and feminist-centered values, Crescendo: The Tampa Bay Women's Chorus is an inclusive women's chorus committed to the performance of music and activities that inspire, educate, and unify." The vision statement further clarifies: "To give voice to the desires and dreams of all people who seek to co-exist in a world of unity and kinship." Sunny Hall was the founding Artistic Director. It is now the oldest lesbian chorus still singing in the Southeast.

With the gay men's chorus, Crescendo co-hosted the Tampa Bay Gay and Lesbian Film Festival in its beginning days. The festival has grown to become the largest film festival of its kind in the United States.

In addition to performing one or two major concerts each year as well as several smaller community events, Crescendo has produced local concerts of Sweet Honey in the Rock, Cris Williamson and Tret Fure, Cris Williamson, Lea DeLaria, Nuru, and Suzanne Westenhoefer. In 2009, they performed with Cris Williamson. Community outreach has included such activities as Adopt a Highway, Paint Your Heart Out, and songwriting workshops for the women of the local spouse abuse shelter. Proceeds from recent concerts go to support local organizations dedicated to eradicating abuse in all its forms. The chorus also takes an active part in the yearly Take Back the Night event, and the Hillsborough County Martin Luther King Jr. Interfaith Memorial Service. Crescendo is online at crescendosings.org

Photo by Don Daly

Crescendo performing at GALA Choruses Festival in 2008
(used with permission of DonDalyPhoto.com).

GINGER STARLING AND OTHER VOICES: THE RICHMOND LESBIAN AND GAY CHORUS

Rose Norman

Songwriter, choral director, keyboardist for the rock band Wicked Jezabel, owner of North Star Piano, a piano servicing business, Ginger Starling grew up in the Deep South (Cuthbert, GA, near the Alabama line), and earned a bachelor's degree in Music Composition. What changed the direction of her life was attending the Southern Baptist Theological Seminary, Louisville, KY, where she earned a Master of Divinity degree in 1987. She recently moved from northern Virginia to Abbeville, AL, to care for her aging parents, after a long career during which she was Artistic Director of Other Voices: The Richmond Lesbian and Gay Chorus (1996–99), as well as playing in several bands. I interviewed her by phone on January 11, 2016.

Rose: It's surprising to me that you would find a Southern Baptist seminary so broadening.

Ginger: I didn't know this when I chose it, but the Louisville Seminary was the most progressive of the six Southern Baptist seminaries. It was all about academic integrity. You could arrive there with a worldview and leave with it intact, but probably not, if you were really paying attention. And my world view really needed shaking up. Going there was probably one of the best things I've ever done for myself. I did leave Christianity after that, but it was a place of really unpacking everything I had brought there with me in terms of prejudices and world view and what I thought the world was supposed to be like. Because it was Baptist, I trusted the process, and the people there, even though I didn't agree with them politically at the time, or didn't understand them at the time. There was just enough of a comfort zone that it allowed me to question. It challenged me to question, but it also gave me a safe place in which to do it. It was a great experience, and I wouldn't trade it for anything.[1]

Rose: What took you to Virginia?

Ginger: I moved to Richmond, VA, because a number of seminary friends lived there. I went there to look for work and to try to figure out being a lesbian. Now for the first time, I had decided that's who I was, and I was going to really learn about this. That really opened up not only a sexual orientation journey of exploration and discovery, but also new pathways of spirituality, new pathways of political expression and feminism. All of these things came out as one for me.

I went to work for the [Southern Baptist] Foreign Mission board when I first came to Richmond in 1987, and in 1991 Other Voices was started. The AIDS epidemic was sort of a catalyst for gay and lesbian choruses all over the land. That epidemic started in the early and middle part of the decade, and I got to Richmond at the end of that decade. There was rumor, there was talk of there being places that had these choruses, and why shouldn't we have one, too. Washington, DC, had a gay and lesbian chorus, and that was the seed, the impetus, the inspiration for the Richmond group to get started. We started out in a church basement. We were not performing publicly for quite a while. This became a place where people wanted to come and be themselves. If you were a woman with a lower voice, and didn't want to sing alto, you felt free to sing tenor, or to try bass or baritone. You were welcome to do it. That was one of the freedoms this group offered, a place to be completely yourself.

Rose: You began by composing for Other Voices. Would you rather have composed for a women's chorus?

Ginger: I liked working with an LGBT Chorus because, for me, at the time, it was very interesting musically to work with all the

---

1 As it turned out, her years there were at the end of the Louisville Seminary's progressive culture. The Southern Baptist church was undergoing a deep change toward ultra-conservatism that her professors did not see coming.

voices, both male and female voices. In our concerts, we would have songs with all voices, and then break out a couple of pieces with just men, and a couple of pieces with just women. It was nice cross-pollination in that sense. It also helped to be in touch and somewhat active during the AIDS crisis. Everybody was affected by it, but with men in the chorus, we had a lot of direct contact with people who were sick, or whose partner was sick.

Now, if there had been a women's chorus [in Richmond], I would have been part of it and would have enjoyed it. But it's easier to write for the wider range. There was a women's chorus in Washington, Bread and Roses, and I loved going to hear them. But we didn't have enough people to divide ourselves. Richmond is a smallish city. I don't think the community could have supported two separate choruses. That's why this chorus worked for us.

Rose: What was it like to be involved with a chorus that was out enough to have "Lesbian and Gay" in the title?

Ginger: We started out quiet and keeping to ourselves. This was the first time for some of us to be out publicly. Some of us were nervous [about our first concert]. I wondered how it would go, if there would be a backlash, violence, or intimidation. There was none. This was probably 1992, and it went very well. It was lovely to take our rehearsal out and actually have a performance. That was empowering and encouraging, and we were off and running.

Rose: Eventually, you got more publicity. How did that affect members?

Ginger: There were always people in the chorus who wanted that safe space, who wanted to be there and sing, but not have to tell anybody they were not out. At the same time, we were becoming more and more of a public face of the Richmond lesbian and gay community. We wanted to invite lots of people to our concerts, have it be a community event, so it was sometimes tough to accommodate those people who could not be out. What we did was that we usually had our concerts at churches, not in big community halls. In the early years, we asked people not to take photographs of faces, but eventually we decided that was kind of shaming. So we took care that those of us who couldn't be out were shielded. Those who could be out would be on the front page of the Arts section.

We had to sort of grow and learn by doing, what worked for everybody. We tried to govern by consensus. We had a steering committee, but we always brought up issues to the whole chorus for discussion, working out the kinks, and I think we did right well. We had a number of internal tensions, like that around being out. We eventually decided we would only perform in venues where we could use the full name of the chorus. We were never going to truncate the name just to Other Voices, so that people didn't know. I think we became a focal point of community and a point of pride in the community. It was exciting to be in Other Voices at that time, in the mid-1990s. We participated in Pride events. In 1993, we had a banner, and a group of us wore our t-shirts to the 1993 March on Washington. That was empowering and pride-full. It gave people a voice, and opportunities to contribute in ways they might not have been able to do and had wanted to do in their lives.

Our big thing was that we were open to everyone. We identified as the lesbian and gay chorus, but we were open to anyone. I had grown up in churches where there were always mixed choruses.

Rose: What did you do after leaving Richmond?

Ginger: In northern Virginia, I went in search of the music community. It took a little while to get established. Jill Strachan, of the Lesbian and Gay Chorus of Washington, put me in touch with a terrific woman named Tuckey Requa, who happened to be in a band called The Tomboys. I was in that band, and several others before joining Wicked Jezabel in 2004. These bands were all female, *mostly* lesbian. Wicked Jezabel is a touring band. We traveled weekends, just about every weekend, 48–50 weeks a year, over the next ten years.

Rose: Other Voices ended in about 2000 or 2001. What do you think its significance was?

Ginger: Other Voices came along at the end of the choral movement, but it was right at the time that the Moral Majority began its push. We were stuck between Jerry Falwell and Pat Robertson. It was sort of a rolling thing. Many [gay and lesbian] choruses were already established, and some were even in decline. We were needed at that time and place. There are places where that is needed now.

Ginger Starling directing Other Voices, 1995.

Photo courtesy of Ginger Starling

CHANGING THE WORLD[1]

Ginger Starling

She set about to challenge the world; womanly heart, but still just
a girl.
It would be years before she would see nothing would change as
much as would she.

Seeking to make a new day
Willing the world to obey;
Earnest and daring and true—
Not always knowing quite what to do.

[refrain]
We will create tomorrow! Changing the world, we're changing
ourselves.
Shape it with joy and sorrow; not leave our lives to somebody else.

Pushing our limits, fighting our fears; sometimes the smallest step
would take years.
Suddenly, bolted doors opened wide; doors that, before, were
locked from inside.

Standing to make a new day, choosing to forge a new way
Earnest and daring and true: we began learning just what to do.

Never! Not for a moment did we think it would be so hard, so
difficult, never!
You never know just what a dream will demand, or where it will
take you to, never

---

1 Commissioned for the Atlanta Feminist Women's Chorus Tenth Anniversary
Concert, 1995. Published by Yelton Rhodes Music, yrmusic.com, © 1995.

The world expected us to quit and, though there were times we were tempted to, Never!
No turning back, because we're living our lives so the world is a better place to be!

Standing to face the new day
Knowing what stands in our way,
Earnest and daring and true:
This is our work, we know what to do!

[refrain]
We will create tomorrow! Changing the world, we're changing ourselves.
Shape it with joy and sorrow; not leave our lives to somebody else.

We celebrate tomorrow! Changing the world, we're changing ourselves.
Born of our joy and sorrow;
Not leave our lives
Not leave our lives to
Not leave our lives to somebody else.

She set about to challenge the world: womanly heart, no longer a girl.

ELAINE KOLB:
SINGER, SONGWRITER, ACTIVIST

Merril Mushroom

Elaine Kolb is a singer/songwriter who was involved with Womansong Theatre and hosted the first lesbian radio show in Atlanta. Born the second of five daughters, she at first "aspired to be a medical missionary,"[1] then earned a BA in urban studies—the first to be awarded—at SUNY Buffalo, where her activist roles included antiwar, civil rights, and early women's movement. In 1970, she went to Cuba on the third Venceremos Brigade—a coalition of young people, mainly SDS members, working in solidarity with Cuban workers and challenging US policies toward Cuba, including the embargo. Part of her decision to go "was because five radical lesbians would be going." Since at that time, being gay was considered abnormal, and lesbians were very closeted, Elaine hoped "this would give me a chance to connect with politically active women who were out and proud lesbians. When I was ready, I would raise my hand and say, 'Me, too!'"

Alas, this was not to be. The radical lesbians all dropped out because of the homophobia they encountered, but Elaine decided to come out anyway. As a result, her friends from Buffalo shunned her, while other non-lesbians threatened and even assaulted her while they were in Cuba, but she found acceptance and friendship among women from Atlanta, GA. After she returned home, Elaine bought a one-way bus ticket to Atlanta, moved down, and connected with her new friends. She moved into "Rubyfruit Jungle," a Lesbian commune formed by radical leftist dykes who were fed up with the sexism and homophobia of antiwar and civil rights hetero lefties.

---

1 All quotations are from Lorraine Fontana's phone interview with Elaine Kolb on September 4, 2015.

In 1970–71, Elaine became involved with Womansong Theatre, a small group of both straight and lesbian feminists who used songs and skits to communicate a feminist women's point of view on sexual politics. She also got involved with WRFG radio (Radio Free Georgia) and had a show called "Lesbian/Woman." In her words:

> I had to get my 3rd class FCC license, so I was qualified to operate the equipment, because you had to do that. Now back in those days we still used turntables. Remember the vinyl record? [There were] two setups on either side of my chair, and it was possible to queue up the record on the left while playing the one on the right, and you had to remember which switches to turn on or off and which dials to adjust, so you would know which mikes were on. We also used reel-to-reel tape recorders, which could be edited by literally cutting and splicing, very carefully. So that's what I did. I was in charge—I mean I had to watch and make sure that the dials were within the range of what they were supposed to be so we would actually be broadcasting. . . . If you were willing to get your FCC license, they needed people. They were always looking for people to fill in, because it was a skilled job, and it also was required. They had to have someone who was licensed, or they would have to take WRFG off the air.

On her show, Elaine played lesbian songs, tapes from Cuba, and "Masters of War," which included the voice of a Vietnamese woman. She played tapes covering civil rights issues, live and taped music, personal interviews. She covered gay rights parades and rallies. She named names of people and organizations that were hostile to gay and lesbian matters.

But she was primarily a creative artist. She describes what this meant to her:

> If I hadn't calmed down and discovered I was a songwriter and started writing songs, and had the direct experience of that inspiration, I might still be breathing, but I wouldn't be alive. For me the creative outlet was how I managed to

process my emotions. When I was singing, I could put all that emotion into it that I couldn't do directly about what I was feeling or what I had been through. But in sharing it through a song, I could pour all of that into the song and channel it, so that I got some release.

One of her first songs was "Forgotten Women," of which she said:

I already knew as a child that I was weird, and I identified with people in institutions. I would visit a mental hospital, and I was kind of afraid they wouldn't let me back out. I would visit the VA hospital or a nursing home, . . . and I just was horrified that people were kept under such conditions—why? So this was something that was very deep inside me from a very early age. But then what finally happened was after being right in the center of ALFA [Atlanta Lesbian Feminist Alliance], fairly suddenly and quickly, I was not. I experienced being shunned and rejected because of a position that I felt absolutely compelled to take that wasn't popular with the people that I was connected to at that stage. The real key for me was that I visited the women's prison . . . right next to the state mental hospital. . . . Once I had been there, I had to go back, to try to do what I could to help those women and their families.

In 1977, Elaine was stabbed in the back by a stranger, resulting in a spinal cord injury. She expanded the scope of her advocacy to include the disability rights movement. She says of this time:

My whole life changed. Like most people, my identity was based on my appearance, strength, and physical capacities. All of a sudden I was in terrible pain, partially paralyzed, in the hospital for two months, had to use a wheelchair, would never run again, applied for Social Security Disability Income, was denied, appealed, won, and then got accepted into Georgia State University as a graduate student. My training as an activist and loyal friends helped me survive this transition. . . . Disability is not a minority issue. Even if it *is* a minority issue, we're the largest minority. But it's still not really recognized or respected by the real civil rights movement, by most people. . . . Now, either you're born with a disability, or you acquire a disability along the way, or if you live long enough you can be damned sure you're gonna have a disability before you die.

Elaine feels it is important for people to know that she has been scared, vulnerable, and depressed as well as being happy, productive, and successful:

Photo courtesy of Elaine Kolb

Elaine Kolb in 1972, singer, songwriter, and founding mother of ALFA.

The point is to give people hope, and to encourage people to explore the creative outlet which might be the key to helping *them* to find their way through the mess. . . . It's so critical to have at least the hint of the possibility that maybe, just maybe you *will* survive, you *will* make it through this awful time, it *could* happen. . . . There is some kind of a spiritual connection that has been very real for me. . . . It's been a powerful thing, and in some cases it's been the only thing that I could grab ahold of and say I'm here for a purpose, that I feel it's important for me to stay and struggle through this.

FORGOTTEN WOMEN[1]

Elaine Marie Kolb

1. I sing the songs of women who were crushed beneath the burden,
Of empty dreams they couldn't call their own,
Who thought they should be happy with a husband and some children,
In a house they couldn't make their home,
And I sing the songs of women who are lonely and afraid,
To live the lives they wanted for themselves,
People always told them they should feel they were in heaven,
But somehow it seemed much more like hell.

2. I sing the songs of women who are sitting on a barstool,
Who only live to buy another round,
Who are drowning in all the sorrows of empty, gray tomorrows,
Whose lives are lost, 'cause love was never found,
I sing the songs of women who are junkies in the night,
Who sell their bodies for another fix,
They tried to live the high life and found they had to buy life,
And they shoot up just to keep from getting sick.

3. I sing the songs of women who are quietly forgotten,
When they lock the door, they throw away the key,
The doctors call them hopeless, as they drug them into silence,
'Cause pain and fear is their reality,
I sing the songs of women in a lonely prison cell,
Who wonder if they'll ever get paroled,
People just don't see them, as they sit there in the darkness,
Of solitary slowly (oh, so slowly) growing old.

4. I sing the songs of women who are poor and gray and wrinkled,
Who will never have a visitor again,

---

1 Date uncertain, probably 1971 or 1972. "One of my first songs," Kolb says.

Families have forgotten the loving care they've given,
So, they'll rock there, waiting only for the end,
I sing the songs of children who are hungry and in pain,
Their people cannot get them what they need,
For in a world of money, life is sold there in the market,
And a child is just another mouth to feed.

5. I sing the songs of people who have never sung their own songs,
Who have never known a love like you or me,
Who have never known the joy of sharing life together,
And struggling so people can be free,
I sing the songs of women, because I am a woman, too,
And we have been forgotten, all these years,
Alone we sing a sad song—but together, there's a glad song,
The touch of love can wipe away our tears.

When we love ourselves—
When we love each other—
When we love ourselves, we'll have—
Yes, together we'll have—
Much less to fear.

FLASHBACKS OF FLASH SILVERMOON, LESBIAN MUSICIAN IN GAINESVILLE

Flash Silvermoon[1]

In September 1975, I moved to Melrose, Florida, with my then partner and band mate Pandora. This adventure began when I met Corky Culver in Bonnie and Clyde's, a lesbian bar where I worked in New York City. Corky was sent there to find me and get a Tarot reading. She figured it was me because I was wearing rainbow suspenders, a purple lamé scarf, and tails.

By the end of the evening, we were fast friends. Corky waxed poetic and described Melrose in great detail—white sand beaches, orange trees, horses, magic mushrooms, swimming naked. I told her I wasn't ready to move down yet, but my psychic self was already engaged. She said, "I didn't ask you to move. Just come visit!" But there was a part of me that already knew. I was moving South and bye-bye New York City, Hello Mellowrose!

We were basically the first women's band in this area as well as in New York City. There were women playing music here, many of them, but there were no bands per se. We were a bit of a novelty. The music here was more country and folk. We were more rock and blues, Janis Joplin style, some punk music, even some world music then. Our band Medusa was Pandora, Michelle Priceman (our neighbor from the East Village), and myself. The three of us moved down together.

We played gay clubs, from the Melody Club to every permutation of gay bars that there was. We played straight venues like a big bowling alley, The Red Fox Lounge, the Pizza and Brew, and so many more. We played all the little clubs around town, and were drawing a very large female crowd, which one would have thought

---

1 Edited by Barbara Esrig from her interview with Flash Silvermoon, November 22, 2015, then further edited by Flash Silvermoon, who provided the lyrics to her song. This interview is not archived, but Rose Norman's November 12, 2012, interview with Flash Silvermoon and Pandora Lightmoon is archived.

was a good thing. We thought it was a good thing, filling the bars. But many of the places would take me aside and they'd say, "um, I hear you bring in a whole lot of women. And well, we're not sure we want this to be thought of as a gay bar." And I said, "Well, we're not standing up and yelling, 'Everybody be gay.' Some of these women aren't." So we started getting banned from most of the straight clubs.

We played the Florida Feminist Festival in 1975, after doing a major Halloween Fest in New York City with Kay Gardner, who was a long-time musical friend. We drove down to St. Pete with her from New York City, which was quite the road trip for all of us. We played Miami Gay Pride, Orlando, Jacksonville, and the Pagoda in St. Augustine. We played all over the South, and national music festivals as well. Anywhere we could.

In Gainesville we played the Orange and Brew a few times, and we were the first people to play on the stage of the bandshell for the Halloween Ball that year, 1979. This was an extreme honor and coup! Debra David was an activist then, and she was running for Vice President of Student Government. She very much wanted us to play, because we made the program a lot more diverse. However, the other regular group, Student Government Productions (SGP), did not really want us to play at all. When we got there, they said, "Listen, we got a spot for you a half hour before it starts, and we will pay because you have a contract, but we just as soon you pack up and go home!" Yup, that was at the Bandshell where they have giant orchestral concerts now. They couldn't stand that the dykes had power and that anyone was challenging them.

We were all dressed in black capes, and had a caldron with dry ice to make it look quite smoky and very witchy. By that point I was so pissed at the way we were being treated by SGP that I raised my sword with a pomegranate on it and hexed the patriarchy from the stage that night. On Halloween. I know they didn't like that! My spell also included that this stage would be graced by many more women, lesbians, and people of color in the future.

Photo courtesy of Corky Culver

Pandora Lightmoon and Flash Silvermoon of Medusa Muzic, one of the first women's bands in New York City, moved to Melrose, FL, and were the first women's rock band in Gainesville.

In the 1980s, the scene changed and I was finding more acceptance for a while. While Medusa was still together, we were playing all around town. We played in Tallahassee for the Halloween Ball, and at different colleges. I probably played Gay Pride in every city in Florida. In Gainesville we used to play with Abby Bogomolny, Denise Burnsed, and Jane Yii, who had been playing with Nancy Luca, who played with me in Flash and the Flood and recorded my first CD with me in the Tidal Wave Band.

I am sure Medusa was the first band that played at the Pagoda. We played there naked sometimes as it would be so hot. I remember those were the shirtless concerts. We were kind of the house band for quite some time, and whoever came through might use my piano and my PA. I remember doing sound for Holly Near, Alix Dobkin, Teresa Trull, and Anique, who came from Australia. Probably a few others as well. We were ground breakers in the North Florida area for women's music.

My music was lesbian-themed, like "Find Yourself a Real Good Woman Tonight" and "An Army of Lovers Can't Fight Their Way Out of Bed." That was a country song. I had to do a country song for being here, you know. "Redneck Cadillac" was another country song, about what happened to a redneck who mistakenly picked up a drag queen one night!

My music has always been cutting edge, and I was writing punk songs before that genre even existed, like "Take a Picture, It Lasts Longer." That's about having people stare at you as you travel the highways and byways of the world. Also, there was "Hands Off Our Religion, Motherfucker." That was my other punk song that I wrote for Z Budapest when we performed at the first Women's Spirituality Conference in Boston in 1976. We also performed with Kay Gardner there. "Lunar Lullaby" was about the Goddess and her moonlight magic. "Morgan the Pirate" was a lesbian song, about a female pirate who sailed around the world picking up women who needed to be liberated from bad situations.

Otherwise, I actually worked in the bookstore at Gainesville's Women Unlimited cooperative for a year or so. Reading and teaching the Tarot and Astrology was becoming my bigger profession. I also read and taught Tarot at Women Unlimited and helped organize Take Back the Night and many other events. Hopefully, this gives you a little taste of the musical climate in Gainesville in the 1970s for an out lesbian rocker.

Photo courtesy of Flash Silvermoon

Flash Silvermoon rocking as Flash Silvermoon and the Blues Sisters, Omialadora Ajamu and Denise Burnsed, women's night at the University Club, Gainesville's main gay bar, 1990s.

TAKE A PICTURE[1]

Flash Silvermoon

Verse I
Did you ever get the feeling you just landed from Mars
People all around you wonderin' what the hell you are
And you ain't doin' nothin' to make them so alarmed
It's just they never seen the likes of you back home down on the farm

CHORUS
Take a picture it lasts longer baby dontcha look at me that way
Take a picture it lasts longer baby dontcha dontcha know it ain't
polite to stare

VERSE II
Well you don't like my clothes and I don't come from Vogue
And you may be thinkin' you're so genteel when ya look way down
your nose
Oh it's Culture Shock ready or not
Hey I ain't contagious just a bit outrageous

CHORUS
VERSE III
Oh I'm your worst fear and your best fantasy why does it scare you
so just seein' people free
And I ain't done nothin' to make you so upset
Is seein' me the biggest thrill that you ever get????

CHORUS
Take a picture it lasts longer baby don'tcha look at me that way
Take a picture it lasts longer baby dontcha know it ain't polite to stare

---

1 © Goddess Tunes 1975.

MUSIC FOR LESBIANS, A LOVE SPELL
Barbara Ester

Another tale, another "Trail of Dykes"
Connected by root, sprouting and branching
Meeting in mind; engaged, holding, and enfolding
A web of womyn, a common thread
And I, conjuring a lover

"So you sing, what *else* can you do?" It sounded like a come on to me. What did she mean by that? I was intrigued. I had just shared a couple of my own songs in a crowded room of Lesbians taking refuge from the rain in South Florida. I guess I got her attention. She got mine. Bairbre looked like a professional photographer with her 35-mm camera in hand, carefully aiming and snapping photos around the room.

I didn't think much about her until we met several months later. A mutual friend invited us to her weekend gathering to share songs. Bairbre brought humorous political songs about being a Lesbian in patriarchy. She's a good songwriter, I thought, but what else can *she* do? Bairbre was ending a relationship and moved into a house down the street from my apartment. It was a good opportunity to meet and get to know each other. We began spending evenings together sharing our views on Lesbians, feminism, and politics. My dyke sensibility sparked as we found a common thread in a Lesbian-only focus. We went dancing at Blackie's, the local women's bar, and our bodies sparked. Lying under the full moon, touching, kissing, and urging exploration drew us closer. Our romance strengthened during our drive to the Michigan Womyn's Music Festival that summer of 1979. We became lovers.

When we returned, Bairbre moved in with me. My apartment was a one-room studio, so we decided to look for a larger place to live. We got jobs together cleaning a school building and offices. Bairbre was emptying trash in a real estate office when she spotted an ad for a house to rent in South Miami. She called, and the next thing we knew, the realtor had convinced us to buy the house. Check my credit, job history; provide the down payment—that's all we had to do. We worked several jobs to raise the money and moved in the following year.

> Music emerged as we merged
> Inspired by the momentum
> Of "pure lust" and love
> "Spilling over," sounding loudly
> Creating ritual and gifts of song

Our home became a comfortable place to make music boldly and loudly. We played our instruments—clarinet, trumpet, harmonica, piano, and guitar—and wrote songs. We gathered friends as easily as we gathered cats and dogs. We had time to be creative. The Friday Night Women's Group sponsored "A Womyn's Concert" in December 1983, and I was on the program. It was the first time we shared our songs. We were well received, so we kept writing. In February 1985, we decided to have a gathering for several weekends. We built a fire pit and a camping area in the vacant lot next door. We called it "A Coven of Lesbian Music." Dyke friends came to our home to share food, sing, and drum around the bonfire. Some of our friends kept asking for more of it, more songs about Lesbians, more songs about our lives. Did we have a recording?

Opportunities to perform came easily as Lesbians opened gathering places for women around Miami. With each performance our audience grew, and dykes continued to request our music. We decided to make a recording of our songs. I gathered information about tape recorders and purchased recording equipment. In 1987 we created our music label, Music for Lesbians. One of my songs on the album included our friends singing in a rousing chorus, "*I'm a Lesbian.*" It was exciting! Using my list of contacts and with the help of friends, we distributed our first recording, "More of It," with ease and received glowing support in letters and reviews.

In an interview in the *Informher*, Miami's Lesbian newsletter, we shared these thoughts: "Our comfort level is geared to self-love," and "Our politics of Lesbian music is a different ladder of success." Our intention for our music is that it be heard by only Lesbians. Our communities, alive and well, still thrive in our hearts and memories.

> *Supportive, interweaving stories*
> *Making time, in rhythm, in song*
> *Dreaming on to our place and other inspirations*
> *Day to day and still grounded in the music*

The Friday Night Women's Group concert, April 15, 1988, Barbara Ester (left) and Bairbre (pronounced "Barbara").

EGO, VANITY AND FRIENDS, A LESBIAN PERCUSSION GROUP

Martha Ingalls

Ego, Vanity and Friends, we call ourselves, a group of lesbian percussionists that over the years has resonated the passion of many cultures. Some share the rhythm for one night, and others' participation spans two decades. We gather not to perform pre-conceived structural melodies and rhythms but to create them spontaneously, instinctively and intuitively. I know I will drum again with the lesbians at Something Special—an experience that will root my feet in the ground and send my soul flying.

I wrote that description of Ego, Vanity and Friends in 1997 for Barbara Ester's *Day to Day* recording with Ego, Vanity and Friends at Something Special in Miami. There should be a herstorical marker at Something Special that reads: On this spot from 1987–2011, F. Louise Griffin and Maryanne Powers served food and fun to women from all over the world. Something Special, located in Liberty City, was a lesbian owned and operated, women-only, vegetarian restaurant and gathering place, with lesbians being the majority of the patrons.

The cultural mix of Miami peppered with transient lesbian travelers created a never-ending flow of lesbians at Something Special. And the instruments we played and the beats we created reflected that spicy mix. Ego, Vanity and Friends and the Something Special experience in its entirety were the ultimate blending of worldly cultures—both dominant and subcultural, vegetarian and carnivore, rich and poor—both spiritually and economically. And that I think is the essence of lesbian culture, a blending of many with the common bond of women loving women.

Ego, Vanity and Friends created rhythm from the late 1980s through 2011. Nestled in Miami's notorious Liberty City,

Something Special raised the vibration of the neighborhood with its laughter, song, and rhythm, and served its food, always, with love. Venturing to Something Special required courage on the part of some women who would have never crossed economic and/or racial boundaries into the inner city of riots, drugs, and poverty except to be with "their kind."

SOUTHERN LESBIAN FEMINIST ARTISTS AND CRAFTSWOMEN

Merril Mushroom

Southern lesbian craftswomen created their own community through networking, artistry, craftswomanship, feminism, and activism—a community based on Southern lesbian values of support, affirmation, cooperation, equity, human rights. Networking was the key to finding opportunities in one's craft, and an essential part of networking was the festival circuit, especially so in the days before electronic communication. Festivals were the primary places where lesbian craftswomen got support and affirmation, and were a primary means for communication and networking with each other.

Robin Toler, herself an artist, interviewed nine Southern lesbian artists and craftswomen about their work created in the last part of the twentieth century.[1] Who are these Southern Lesbian Feminist artists and craftswomen? By and large, as Toler writes:

They are alternative individualists; unconventional, emotionally driven, always questioning. They were often politically aware and motivated to make changes in social policy and practices. Southern lesbian artists were often called pushy, aggressive, unfeminine, and dykeish; they were known as demanding, obnoxious, and loud. They challenged the status quo. They crafted their own role, . . . being true to yourself on one hand and making items of art that would

---

1 Robin Toler conducted interviews with the following Southern artists and craftswomen: Jenna Weston (Hawthorne, FL, June 10, 2015), Mary-Ellen Maynard (Canon City, CO, September 21, 2015), Daphne Mushatt (Baton Rouge, LA, August 14, 2015), Turtle Girl (Metairie, LA, September 3, 2015), Victoria Singer (Nashville, TN, August 19, 2015), Phyllis Free (Atlanta, GA, July 14, 2015), Susan LosCalzo (Rutherfordton, NC, June 27, 2015), Phyllis Parun (New Orleans, LA, November 20 and 25, 2015), Joa March (Gainesville, FL, July 6, 2015). All were conducted by phone. Unless otherwise noted, all quotations are from these interviews. Rose Norman's October 16, 2015, interview with Phyllis Free is also archived.

sell and generate income on the other hand. . . . Many had to hide their identities. . . . They had fluency of ideas; they were playful and innovative; they were divergent thinkers. They were resourceful, . . . had tremendous strengths, and broke many social expectations. . . . Some identified fully as an artist; some didn't see themselves as an artist at all. . . . They were feminists with feminist ideals, values, influencing their work, life, and relationships. They were spiritual beings, lesbian-identified, and goddess worshipping.[2]

Lesbian artists and craftswomen who were making it into mainstream markets often were required to hide their identities as lesbians. Remember, this was a time when homosexuality was not only illegal but considered to be immoral as well. An artist's career could be derailed and ruined by outing her.

The women Toler interviewed discussed the differences in defining art and craft. Jenna Weston spoke of crafts as being useful and utilitarian, involving a variety of materials like fiber, fabric, pottery, glass, and said that crafts are associated with women and poor people. Arts she described as more idea related, more cerebral, less physical. People tend to pay more for things that are not functional. Thus crafts that may have their origins in utilitarianism then become decorative. Weston noted that crafts were considered less valuable because they were traditionally associated with women, home, children. Art was related to abstract ideas, and art by men often commanded a higher price.

Financial survival was and is difficult. Many lesbians had to keep mainstream jobs in order to support their craft. Marketing one's product could be too time-consuming to do adequately. A few had support from family or friends, but most artists did not have enough economic stability. Some gave classes to supplement their incomes. Some had support from partners, and sometimes this led to feelings of inequality in the relationship. The costs of

---

2 Quoted from Toler's unpublished notes about these interviews.

maintaining the right credentialing to get into mainstream shows is a real burden that takes a tremendous amount of time, energy, and resources. Then, artists had to be ready to engage in public/private interface—making art is a private experience; showing art is a public practice.

Representational art and craft reflected lesbian spirituality, and much of it celebrated seasons, rites of passage, and other transitions. Much was intertwined with nature/expressive of the goddess. Many lesbians used their art/craft to heal from social, emotional, or sexual trauma. They also used their art/craft in political activism. Weston accurately places lesbian art in political perspective, its purpose being "to counteract the destructiveness and ugliness of patriarchal culture, to create things of beauty and engage in political activism."

HOW I BECAME
A SOUTHERN LESBIAN FEMINIST ARTIST

Robin Toler

If there is one thing I have come to know about being a Southern lesbian artist, it is not easy to become one. Well, at least it was not easy for me. To become a Southern lesbian artist, I thought first you had to have a tragic beginning. My mother's absence cultivated my artistic development, encouraged me to live fully, and set a dramatic example of what not to do. Her death, so unexpected and shocking, cast a huge shadow over my early beginnings.

Her non-being became larger than life, exceeding my imagination in struggle, rejection, and invisibility. My mother's paintings, like the prints of Picasso, Chagall, and Klee, lined our large country home. After her eighth child, after experiencing severe post-partum depression, after seventeen years of marriage built on aggression and violence, my mother, at thirty-nine completed suicide. I was six. Ten years later, my father died.

Born into a big Catholic extroverted family in rural Louisiana, I felt like the lone introvert. While my mother was alive, I attended private school. After her death, I went to public school. As a member of an upper-middle-class family, I was active in plays, dances, woodshop, 4-H, and Girl Scouts. My father taught me to make things, to develop film, and fly his airplane. He taught me how to be a woman and what to expect from men—setting my development in motion. After being orphaned, I drifted. I lived with more than fifteen different people, and at age eighteen, I made my way even with nowhere to go. The Southern women I knew were trapped in a male-dominated landscape with male institutions dictating their roles. I knew there was something more, but that something was not yet visible.

My first successful painting was of my brother in the US Army (pinks and turquoise). My second painting showed how I looked at women with the classic male gaze. I painted a woman greeting a man in a garden on the verge of love, romance, and pleasure. As a young woman, expressing myself with paintings and sketches, I drew the human body attempting connection and curious exploration: many nudes. As a child and young woman, I was punished for natural creative expression and got in trouble at school. Drawing faces with different expressions, I was recommended for psychological help, and spent time in foster care.

The choices, freedoms, and warmth I wanted were in conflict with being told I was overweight, unattractive, and stupid. I felt ostracized, excluded, and overruled. With my hands, I made things; with my mind, I began to write fiction and memorize poems. When old enough, I rebelled, bought a motorcycle, and began to drink. I recited all the sayings women and girls tell each other to keep themselves in line under patriarchal rules. In college, I took formal art classes—exhilarating, stimulating, and expressive—prompting a minor in art. My only female art teacher encouraged me to go to graduate school in art therapy.

Through art I could process the brutality and reality of being female: assault by family members, rape by family friends, rape by men I dated. At nineteen I was gang-raped. I realized then that the things I was told about being safe were untrue. Art cut through what I was taught. I lived in a world of hurt, confusion, and anger. Unsure of what I was expressing or experiencing, I used art to express the inexpressible. Drawing my own female nakedness, I tried to make sense of my body as it existed in a hostile, violent world. Art organized my experiences and provided a context for healing my mind–body split. Art saved me.

In 1986 I got sober, and in 1990 I started graduate school, kept a journal, and made art. I studied my own art intensely and, being good at art assessment and analysis, I studied the art of others—academically. In graduate school I worked at a domestic violence resource agency, suddenly surrounded by strong, knowledgeable, and gutsy feminists. Many were lesbians. They taught me about feminism, social justice, and women's issues. I learned to make rituals, build personal traditions, and learn about diversity and health. I was taught about violence against women, the value of political activism, and human rights.

Learning about power imbalances, I looked at men, their social institutions and organizations from a new perspective; male privilege and power, once uncovered is quite hard to overlook. Rethinking my place in the world, I moved back to Louisiana in 1994, making masks, painting eggs, building sculptures, and exploring the decorative arts. I gave workshops on women's issues: grief and loss, motherless women, creativity, deciphering personal symbols, women and substance abuse recovery, and women's story dolls. I taught classes, gave workshops, and built support for women through art and creativity.

My development, like my art, explored controversial ideas and social processes: heterosexism, poverty, oppression, spirituality, and sexuality. My partners were not helpful. I got pregnant at thirty-four, and it was complicated. I made art around the experience of being pregnant and terminating the pregnancy—a turning point in my life. After that, I struggled to find my tribe, women who lived in a subversive social club, women with heightened consciousness, some budding feminists, a network of like-minded women who were revolutionary, politically active, and mostly invisible, but they were not artists.

As my career grew, I realized I could not apply feminist therapy practices while employed in a medical facility where an image of a woman's thigh in a patient's art project prompted a write-up in my employment file. I learned much about misogyny and sexism sitting in meetings where well-educated medical people laughed at women for sex work/prostitution, drug addiction, rape, domestic violence, and poverty. It was infuriating and disgusting. This prompted me to begin my own private art therapy and addictions counseling practice where I incorporated feminists values and therapy skills, and counseling techniques with traditional art therapy.

I continued to make my life experiences more conscious through art, to work with others in therapy, and I began to have art shows. However, my pieces were often censored: I was told to "tone it down" and "please don't show that one." I felt ambivalence about my vulnerability in showing art pieces on controversial real-life topics: recovery from incest, sexual assault, and addiction recovery. My art was about reclaiming parts of being female living in patriarchy. My art was about empowerment, agency, and freedom. There were no lesbian feminist art projects in my area and much of my art was hidden from my family. When I did put feminist art products out in the public, almost inevitably I was asked to take them down.

Art created by Southern lesbians shows body images of women that are more realistic and natural, frequently resulting in a structurally larger, plumper physical shape. This was a connection with the divine feminine, or Goddess spirituality. By drawing the female form and making female imagery central to the design and composition, the artist takes ownership. It is a form of identity, a rite of passage, and a personal stamp of increased activism and increased consciousness, reflecting my own growth and development as an artist and lesbian. When I showed art in Mississippi, Louisiana, Texas, Tennessee, and Georgia, the space always set the tone for the show. Being obligated to follow venue guidelines as a tradeoff to exhibit art, I did what I could to get my art out in public. At thirty-eight, my art had preceded my coming out. I had no role models, templates, or gurus. I learned by doing.

Rejection, isolation, discrimination, and failures accentuated my development—the loss of sales, the presentations that flopped, the jobs I lost; the book I wrote that tumbled, the shows I did not get in for one reason or another—all fueled my career path. Womonwriters at the Southeastern Lesbian Writing Conference helped clarify who I was and who I am. The women there allowed me to acknowledge and take pride in my diverse skill set as an artist, writer, and healer. Because of discrimination, loss of sales, and missed opportunities to exhibit, my written artist statements did not identify me as "lesbian."

Today my art and activism promote personal authenticity and transparency. Professionally, I am focused on health, cultural competency, diversity, and Focused Four: Racism, Violence Against Women, Poverty, and LGBTQ issues. I have donated pieces to LGBTQ centers and feminist bookstores. You can find my artwork at the Louisiana State University Women and Gender Studies office and library, the Women's Center at LSU, Tau Center, Our Lady of the Lake Regional Medical Center and Baton Rouge General Hospital, the Baton Rouge Shaw Center, as well as in private collections across the country. In 2015, I was honored by the Louisiana Division of the Arts, and listed on the official Louisiana Artist Roster.

Photo courtesy Robin Toler

Artist, Robin Toler, in 2015, at her home studio office. Toler is active in the Southern Lesbian Herstory Project. Her paintings are featured on the covers of this issue as well as *Sinister Wisdom* 93 and 98.

My journey as a Southern lesbian artist started in tragedy. Now it is a celebration. My art is personal and political. I am proud to be a part of a special group of Southern lesbian artists who are not yet well known, who are intensely passionate, who have paid their dues to be free, and to live bold, extraordinary, and courageous lives.

SUE PARKER WILLIAMS, AKA RAINBOW
Merril Mushroom

Rainbow was born in Shreveport, LA, in 1934 and grew up there in "...a very racist, homophobic, sexist family—just normal Southern folks."[1] She began with her art as a toddler when she entertained herself by drawing on whatever paper she could find. She began to be aware of racism expressed by her family around the age of five. She says, "I had a family that gave me something to differentiate from, so I would become OTHER, which is uncomfortable, but I think an ARTIST has to do that. You can make bolder decisions when you're out of the loop, not seeking approval."[2]

Throughout grade school and high school, Rainbow felt a preference for girls and women, but she didn't act on it until decades later. She says of herself, "I BLOOMED LATE and WILL LAST LONG." She graduated from the University of Arkansas in 1955 with a degree in art, married a man, and went traveling. In 1964, they went to live in Mexico and study crafts—clay, weaving, batik, silversmith, bronze forging, woodworking, painting, printmaking. They moved back to Florida to teach crafts, and Rainbow did wax resist silk batik. In 1969, Rainbow officially came out as a lesbian.

Over the next eight years, she worked in clay. She and her then lover created a pottery studio and shop in her carport and built a kiln and wheel from scratch. Then she wanted to focus on woodworking, specifically dulcimer making. Her new lover became a dulcimer player, and, over the years, Rainbow has made thirty-seven dulcimers and taught herself how to play.

---

1 From Rose Norman's interview with Rainbow, November 9, 2013, at Rainbow's home and gallery in St. Augustine, FL. All quotations are from this interview unless otherwise noted.

2 Rainbow heavily edited the notes quoted here from her interview. The use of all caps is a stylistic choice of hers, as is the capitalization of *Lesbian*.

In 1977, she went to her first National Women's Music Festival (the fourth NWMF), "and found everything. I learned from Holly Near how to use music to raise consciousness in a very pleasant way, to build community. Ginni Clemmens taught how to do a circle go around, get everyone to participate. I came home and was part of starting *CHANGES*, which was our local newsletter. . . . Two of us started Lavender Bookmobile, a lending library, mostly Rita Mae Brown. In 1978 I created THE AMAZING ALMOST ALL GIRL STRING BAND, two artists and two Lesbians who could sing or play some outrageous feminist materials."

Photo by Sarah Carawan

Rainbow posing in front of a piece she showed at the 1982 opening of the Orlando Women in Art House. Her piece was a three-mirror dresser, with a bunch of tiny musicians and a hidden tape recorder playing Kay Gardner music. The piece also appears in the *Women Spirit* spring equinox issue (1982), with essays by Jo Jordan, Penny Villegas, and Susan Glaise.

Photo by Benson Williams

Rainbow at 82, in front of her traveling bakers rack show, exhibited at many places, including Silver Threads, Wild Iris Bookstore, Melrose Coffee Shop, and Shake Rag Gallery. It now lives in her dining room.

Her art always was filled with women and goddesses. "I need the blessings to keep me flying," she says. By the early 1980s she had moved to a house in Orlando. She found a bigger garage studio space where she could make larger wooden sculpture assemblages. There, she produced a show of some locals coordinated with a national GREAT AMERICAN LESBIAN ART SHOW (GALAS). Among other pieces were open-face guitars with personal stuff inside and another piece with a copy of [Jill Johnson's] *LESBIAN NATION* inside a hinged door. She says about putting pieces within pieces, "When you can open a box, window, or door, you can put propaganda inside. Art instantly becomes political."

In 1978, Rainbow began spending time at the Pagoda, a women's community in St. Augustine, FL, and in 1984, she moved there permanently. She has done a scale drawing of the Pagoda properties and a mural of the residents. When she was fifty, she met Dore Rotundo, an architect, and apprenticed with her for the next three years. They designed and built a beach house at Pagoda. In 1983, "I was accepted in a Women's Studies program in LESBOS, GREECE led by Carol P. Christ that has continued to inspire me, particularly my writing, but also in creating MUSIC as Sappho did. She had a lyre, I had a dulcimer!" In 1984 she joined the Gainesville to Key West Peacewalk, and in 1985 she went to Australia to meet with artists and peace activists. In the early 1990s, she took her art to Canada and the northeastern United States, as well as the Southeast. Throughout her travels, there always were wonderful women, and sometimes A Wonderful Woman.

Today Rainbow lives in a house by the river where she has a permanent art collection and archives,[3] open to the public by appointment. She sold her Pagoda house and no longer travels. She says, "IT'S GOOD, LIFE AT EIGHTY."

---

3 Rainbow has posted a twelve-minute studio tour on YouTube at Rainbow Williams Archives.

GATHERING ROOT BASKETRY

Jenna Weston

When my partner and I moved to an old farm in the Missouri Ozarks in 1985, I knew I needed a way to make money that was outside of mainstream employment. The nearest town (population 2000) was twenty-five miles away, and I would have been lucky to find even a minimum-wage job there. So I decided to start a small cottage industry making baskets. Gathering Root Basketry began in a 12′ × 24′ studio built with the help of a grant from Lesbian Natural Resources (LNR). LNR funded self-sufficiency projects created by landdykes.

Before coming to the farm, I had learned to weave traditional Appalachian-/Ozarks-style containers, such as double-bottomed ribbed egg baskets and rectangular plaited garden baskets. After several months at the farm, I had made enough inventory to sell my wares at the first of many crafts fairs. I began to add more of my own touches to the traditional basket designs. Some of the weaving materials were colored with natural dyes that I brewed from walnut hulls, onion skins, and sumac berries, which were grown on or gathered from the land.

Enlisting the aid of my horse, Gray Cloud, I foraged near and far for my supplies. I would ride to different locations, tie my horse to a tree, and harvest materials I needed. From tall trees in the woods, I pulled down wild grapevines, and braved poison ivy and chiggers to acquire honeysuckle overgrowing old fence rows. These were bundled and lashed behind my saddle, and I rode back home with my finds. The wild materials would then need to be trimmed, boiled, stripped, and coiled before they could be used to construct a basket.

Although much physical labor was involved in my handmade enterprise, it was satisfying work. The profits were never great, but along with money brought in by my partner, who did rural peoples' taxes, we were able to get by. We also grew and preserved much of our own food, leading a basic, frugal lifestyle.

In time, my background in fine arts began asserting a need for more creativity. I added new items to my inventory, such as handwoven "ritual rattles" and free-form vessels that were more sculptural than functional. Later I even incorporated handmade paper.

Photo courtesy of Jenna Weston

Jenna Weston
and baskets, 1990s.

Over the years I produced many hundreds of baskets, selling at craft shows and women's festivals all over the country. Sometimes in my travels I would walk into the homes of lesbians I had never met and find one of my creations in their kitchen or hanging on a living room wall. I like to think my baskets carried some of the energy of their earth origins to each of the people who took them home.

CREMATION URN IN THE PEACE GARDEN AT SUGARLOAF WOMEN'S VILLAGE

Harvest

I visited Sugarloaf Women's Village for the first time in 2010. Meeting Bonnie Netherton via email on the *Maize* google group and hearing some of the land's herstory from Sally Willowbee inspired me to fly south to Key West. Sally had known Blue Lunden and has many connections with the land.[1]

I stayed in the community house at Sugarloaf. The land was blooming with flowers, all new to me. Bonnie made the community house welcoming and colorful. She told me that Ruth Dreamdigger had lived there and died there. Ruth liked dragons. She and other sisters of the land are memorialized in the Peace Garden, a sacred place in a wooded corner of the land. I spent quiet time there honoring sisters gone ahead (as my mother put it).

Many womyn worked to create the peace garden. Bonnie and Xylena made the paths. Morgana made the urn. Sandy Hagan and Barbara Vogel built the roof and coral base for the urn. This beautiful big ceramic sculpture is decorated with a dragon for Ruth, doves for Barbara, and a mermaid for Blue.

So much of our herstory in this special place, this few acres, this quiet garden! To have a special place, a garden of remembrance to honor these lesbians who worked and struggled before us— what a gift! In my bones I know they are my ancestors.

---

1 See Rose Norman, "Sugarloaf Women's Village: 'Some Ground to Stand on,'" *Sinister Wisdom* 98 (Fall 2015): 63–73. Blue Lunden inherited the Sugarloaf land from Barbara Deming and Jane Verlaine, and left it to a women's land trust. The land trust allows women to become permanent residents or visitors.

Photo by Bonnie Netherton

Cremation urn from the Sugarloaf Peace Garden. Pottery by Morgana MacVicar. Bonnie Netherton writes: "When Blue died in August of 1999, she had not gotten around to finding a final resting place for the ashes of Barbara Deming, Jane Verlaine, Ruth Dreamdigger, and Maua Flowers. I had been asked by Blue's daughter, Linda, to sort through Blue's papers and belongings and help find homes for it all. The ashes of these four beloved women were sitting in boxes on Blue's bookshelves. And now, Blue's ashes also needed a special resting place. In the woods behind her house, there was a bit of a clearing made by Hurricane Georges in 1998, which seemed to me like a lovely spot to create a special 'peace garden' where we could place the ashes in an urn. . . . In February of 2000, all was ready and a dedication ceremony was held."

LOFTY NOTIONS

Merril Mushroom

In 1978, Susan LosCalzo, a radical lesbian-feminist artist in New Orleans, opened a business which she named Lofty Notions. She built sleeping lofts into the high ceilings of homes.

When she was in high school, she would do drawings of houses, but she was discouraged from becoming an architect because she was a woman.[1] While she was teaching, she began making little things out of wood and liked that so much she quit teaching and opened a woodshop called Reflections in Wood where she would sell the items she made. Then a friend asked her to build a loft, and that was the beginning of Lofty Notions. She was covered by the local newspaper and the TV station, and she got a spread in *Better Homes and Gardens* magazine.

When she first started her business, she contacted Angela Hill to congratulate her on becoming the first female news anchor for channel 4 in New Orleans, and mentioned that she herself was also a woman who started her own business. Angela Hill asked Susan for an interview to do a news story and shot some footage of a loft she was in process of building. This resulted in a call from a man who was a sales representative for Rockwell Tools who wanted Susan and her partners to build a loft right there on the show. He gave them a whole shop full of tools, and they built him a loft for his kid. Susan felt that was a good trade. They also got a lot of publicity.

"As a woodworker," she says, "had I not been a feminist, I don't think I would have had the self-esteem to pursue such a nontraditional career, so feminism set that up for me very well . . .

---

1 So was Rainbow Williams (see "Sue Parker Williams," this issue, page __) But see "The North Forty," *Landykes of the South* (SW 98, Fall 2015, p. 19) p. 21, for Dore Rotundo, who became Florida's second woman architect and whose March 20, 2016, interview is archived at Duke as part of the Southern Lesbian Feminist Activist Herstory Project.

the basic ethics and values [were expressed] I was always fair with customers and I tried to make my prices right and I had a bit of a sliding scale … and that is a feminist value."[2]

In 1981, she and her then partner started a women's and children's campout in Pensacola, FL, which has continued to this day. They also had a women's center, a free clothing shop, a bookstore, a women's newsletter (*Distaff*), antiwar marches, and Susan was a distributor for Olivia Records.

Susan LosCalzo of Lofty Notions, routing steps for a loft—a woman at work.

In 1987, she went digging for crystals in Arkansas. In a local rock shop, she bought a set of chakra stones that were put together by Katrina Raphael, plus a book on using stones for healing. She had an intuitive gift for healing and felt a strong affinity for the stones. She read, did research, and acquired crystals and gemstones, and Lofty Notions became a metaphysical rock shop as well as a loft-building business. Eventually, the rock selling took completely over, and Susan retired from building lofts. She operated Lofty Notions as a metaphysical rock shop and did the festival circuit for eighteen years. Then she sold it. The rock shop remains in business but with a different name.

---

2 All quotations are from Robin Toler's phone interview with Susan LosCalzo, June 27, 2015.

LESBIAN FEMINIST VISUAL ARTISTS IN GAINESVILLE, FL

Barbara Esrig, Robin Toler, and Rose Norman

Gainesville and Melrose, FL, have a lively arts community. Among their popular and prolific lesbian visual artists are Pyramid Chainsaw, Joa March, and Lorelei Esser.

Pyramid Chainsaw interviewed by Barbara Esrig

Pyramid is hardly a stranger to anyone who has gone to Michfest as well as most other women's festivals. Born in Zurich, she headed for the United States at an early age. Here is her earliest memory of it:

> Yes, I actually was gonna leave home when I was five, me and my boyfriend. But we were gonna go to America on our three-wheel little bicycles, and that was my initiation. We drove probably for almost two miles down one of the main roads in Zurich, and we were going to America. He was getting stuck in those rain guards, those metal rain guards that were part of the street and part of the sidewalk, and so I was blaming him at the time that he wouldn't make it to America because he took too much time. The cops saw us and came, and my father, who happened to be home that weekend, came in his giant gigolo Plymouth, which was the only American car probably in that neighborhood that we knew of. That was actually the first time that I got smacked, that I remember. And I remember us flying onto the back seat, our three-wheel bicycles lying on the back seat, and me coming home and my mother, who is not a drama queen at all, saying: "In America! She wanted to go to America!"[1]

---

1 All Pyramid quotations are from Barbara Esrig's interview with her on June 29, 2015, in Gainesville, FL.

In a nutshell, that's Pyramid. Always full of amazing stories. It was Pyramid who came in the middle of the night when I was in ICU after my terrible car accident to tell me sex stories, and yes, I credit those stories and loving laughter as a definite part of my fast healing! She rebukes labels, saying "*I see myself as a reuser rather than an artist.*" Her infamous haircuts, the wavy roof on her totally self-built house, her clothes pins, her outrageous dyke fashion shows, her painted walls and colorful dildo straps, her private art show extravaganzas in Europe, and her always deep listening make up part of who we all know as Pyramid.

Photo by Sandy Malone

Pyramid's home, her largest art piece. She built this one-room structure entirely by herself, every nail, every board, every stroke of paint.

Pyramid: I came to Gainesville in 1988, and Sandy Malone immediately invited me to park my van at her house. My dog was welcome. Gainesville already was an art scene, very much an art scene going on. But it wasn't my style. It was too earthy and too conventional. I heard that in Gainesville the women were organizing an anti-nuclear disarmament march from Gainesville to Key West. And that was up my alley. I came to Florida. But my scene was actually lesbian art at the festivals.

Barbara: How would you describe your art?

Pyramid: Well, I was more neon metallic . . . glittery . . . angles, sort of abstract. I wasn't blocked in. My first couple years here, maybe three years, I was very poor. Before I actually had to work, I tried to create. So I did some fashion shows here. I did some auctions.

Barbara: Fashion shows?

Pyramid: Well, a lot of women would comment on my clothing, on my style, so I thought, well, if I could do something, a lesbian event. It was quite elaborate, including a few dykes involved as models. Something light hearted, but that women would pay to come see. I never really made money on those events, but I started having a table there to sell things that I made, photographs of my art and postcards or clothespins, and so on. And since we were in the later 1980s the whole sex revolution among lesbians started exploding.

So some would do the runway. Lesbians were on either side, and some of it was very provocative and sexy, and I think that's what we were about. I would have some things that I created or made. Or transformed, you know? And auction those items maybe during one of the intervals. And that was basically the money I would make from the event.

Barbara: And what were some of the things you were selling?

Pyramid: Some things I transformed—literally I picked up some cool pieces of furniture in thrift stores, painted, some wood carving with a hot iron thing. I painted trash cans, mailboxes. Maybe I had a couple cool mirrors at times. Broke all the mirrors and glued them onto these things. My toilet seats have always been a hit. My painted clothespins, as bizarre as it sounds, was always a hit.

And then once my leather fashion came, partly because of sex revolution and evolution, I started doing leather and dildo straps, because there was the need and the want out there, and the only access at that time was the black leather of men's [sex] toy stores. Some would have worn a leather dildo strap, if it wasn't black leather. And I wasn't willing and able to pay already at that time sixty, seventy, ninety dollars for a dildo strap that didn't really work on my body. So I re-invented myself and took a chance on learning something new. And the feedback was so positive.

Barbara: Were you selling those mostly in festivals?

Pyramid: Uh hum. At festivals and then sometimes at communities I was visiting.

Barbara: How did you get the leather?

Pyramid: The leather, first, because it was so new, it was thrift store belts and things, then at hardware stores. Because I loved colors, and I just thought to take any of those "isms" away from

Photo by Sandy Malone

dildo straps, from leather, let's make it colorful, playful. If we associate playful with colors, or colors with playfulness, then half of the job is done. And that maybe also could help to step over some stereotypes and over some "isms." I think I succeeded to a degree over fifteen years. And that's a very cool thing to say. So, you know, what am I? Am I an artist? I think I'm an entrepreneur. I'm a recycler.

Pyramid.

Joa March interviewed by Robin Toler[2]

Joa March and her life partner Carmen Rose have been creating fun and functional works of art in Gainesville since 1992. "FUN-iture" is what they term the furniture art they create,

---

made with found pieces of furniture embellished with ceramic tile, wood, upholstery, and paint.

Robin: Tell me about your identification as an artist.

Joa: All my life I wanted to be an artist. I had planned to go to art school, but my parents both died of cancer by the time I was seventeen, and I didn't have the money. I became addicted to their morphine as I cared for them at home. I graduated from high school in New York and never went back. I came out, lived on the streets, drinking and using drugs. Then I got pneumonia, and I needed to move south, drawn by the Pagoda to Florida. It was 1980, and I was thirty. I would make art and sell my art on the street. I ended up on the streets for three years. I have been sober since 1983, and living in Gainesville for thirty-two years. This is where Carmen Rose and I met.

Photo by Joa March

HELLO GORGEOUS written on the mirror speaks for itself, reflecting self-love and admiration, and a reminder every time someone looks in the mirror. Joa has been making these mirrors since 1991.

Robin: What was the role of your partners in your work as an artist?

Joa: They have been supportive and encouraging. I moved down to Florida from Vermont in a school bus with Morgana, my partner at the time. She was a musician, and she played music, and I sold art on the streets of St. Augustine. But Carmen, my partner of twenty-five years and now wife, has not only been real supportive but collaborative directly with my art.

Art is something I have to do to have my sanity and to create; it is not always about the money, but about creating beautiful things. I consider myself a colorist; I love vibrant bright colors. I do mirrors with designs around them. One of the mirrors is called "Hello Gorgeous." I did women's art, labryses and female imagery, and peace signs. I want to spread peace around the world. I've done suns, and goddess imagery.

I do a lot of painted dots, as well as tile work, and Carmen paints words. I put mirrors in old window frames—it's recycled, functional, and fun. I do coffee tables, and I collaborate with other artist like Feral [Wilcox]. We did a table, and I did a table with her, and so did Carmen. She painted one side, and I did the other. They were called "cooperation tables."

Robin: Who inspires you?

Joa: Frida Kahlo, and yes, I love Georgia O'Keeffe. She was my favorite.

And what about lesbian artists? They say, "I love you, I love your work, we were supposed to do a trade and we didn't get a chance to give you yours. We love that piece you gave us."

Robin: Were you ever able to support yourself as an artist?

Joa: No, I don't have the marketing skills. I've been a nanny, for money and fun.

Robin: Did you go to festivals?

Joa: I went to the Southern Women's Music & Comedy Festival, and I did sell at Michfest, in the 1980s and 1990s. There were lots of festivals I attended, and sold art by just walking around.

Lorelei Esser interviewed by Rose Norman[3]

Lorelei Esser grew up in Gainesville, FL, and has lived and worked in New York, Europe, and Thailand. She came out in 1972 through the Melrose lesbians and was part of the group who produced the Women's Renaissance Festival in Gainesville in 1974. She is currently a properties designer for the Hippodrome regional theatre in Gainesville. For images and upcoming exhibitions, see loreleiesser.com.

Lorelei: I've always been an artist. This room we're sitting in was the first bedroom built on [to my childhood home], for my brother's and my bedroom. This was a tiny house to begin with. We had been sleeping in the living room on two day couches. Finally, when they built the upstairs, I had my own room here, which was apart from them. The whole room was covered with collage. It was an art piece. I have done that ever since, everywhere that I go.

My art form is found object art. I collect everything. I don't go and buy things for the art. I've got to find it, which takes me on many adventures and travels and journeys. I'm always looking for pieces for the work. I'll see an object, and I'll know what it will become. Other things are just so interesting I have to have them, and later on it's revealed to me what they are. I've always looked at the world that way, visually. I don't see the tree or the house, but the shapes and textures. To me, that has been a great opening, to see past what something is referred to or known as.

My first studio was on University Avenue above Vidal Drugs. I started casting women's breasts. How did I get started in that? I think just the shape was so interesting. I wanted to do a sculpture by putting all these pieces together, a huge globe with these pieces coming out of it. I don't know who the first person was. I didn't cast it as a mold, but used plaster bandages soaked in water and laid on the body (covered with Vaseline) to dry. You can paint right on that.

---

3 Rose Norman interviewed Lorelei Esser at Esser's home in Gainesville on March 21, 2016.

Photo courtesy of Lorelei Esser

Sentinel by Lorelei Esser has this artist statement: "She is the guardian teacher, 'old school' knowledge, plugged in without a cord, wireless without a net, her tools, the pen and the page. Her shield protects the truth, her crown blooms fruitful fancy, and she flies."

When I cast women's breasts, they would talk about them, and I started to take notes. "This one's bigger," "this one's smaller," "my nipples are inverted," or "too big." I would write these down while they were drying. I was surprised at how many women were not happy with their breasts. My mother, when I cast hers, talked about breast feeding. She was a nurse, and she talked about how you had to teach a baby how to nurse. Everyone had their breast stories, and that became a part of it. I built it in that studio.

Interviewer: How did you get women's stories into the art?

I would write on the inside of the plaster. That part isn't always going to be seen. To me, a lot of the things I do, it's there but you don't see it. Most of my work is about the energy of these objects, what they've been through, whose pocket they've been in, who loved it, who shoved it away in a drawer. These things all have a life, and putting them together captures the energy of this story. That's what these breasts were about. Everything I do is about the energy of these things.

In 1993, I had a story and a photo of my art in *Ms Magazine*. They published a photo of the "Under the Sink" part of *Kitchen Box*. (They picked the worst picture to use.) I had done my entire kitchen as an installation. The sandwiches were money sandwiches. The refrigerator was full of poison that you can buy at the grocery store. Someone brought a curator here, and I did a big show at Neptune Beach.

The latest piece that I did started with a piece of siding off of my friends Susan and Bill's house. They know I love materials like this, and they gave it to me. Another piece I found on the road, the sole of a very big shoe. Who walked in those shoes? They walked a lot in them, because they walked part of it off. This is the kind of work I do from found objects.

SHEKERES RULE: THE STORY OF
MARKET WIMMIN AFRICAN CRAFTS

Blanche Jackson

The shekere is a percussion instrument from West Africa made from a dried gourd with beads, seeds, or shells woven into a net covering the outside of the gourd. It is used today throughout the Continent and in the Americas and the Caribbean. When we lived in New York, Amoja Three Rivers and I were taking shekere lessons with an African percussion group. After we left the City, we lived for a time in a rural community. We thought we would like to try making our own shekeres, so we included gourds in the vegetable garden we planted. Making these instruments was not going to be an easy task. We would have to figure out how to cut, gut, clean, and finish the gourds, how to affix the beads, and how to wrap the bottom ring of the beadwork. After much trial and error, we managed to produce six good shekeres, and then ran out of money. We brought the shekeres to an East Coast festival,[1] and sold them all. With the proceeds, we bought food, fishing line, and beads, and then we prepped some more gourds. We wood-burned designs around the tops, burned the Market Wimmin logo on the bottoms, and we were in business!

Market Wimmin's merchandise selection increased through our association with a Nigerian prince. We had gone into a shop in Baltimore that was filled with African goods. The proprietor introduced himself as "Akin," but I noticed that his business card read "Prince Akin." We found out that his father was a chief. Akin would take us into a room and have us sit. He would bring in items one at a time and show them as if we were high rollers. He insisted that we choose what we wanted, anything from drums to dashikis. When we had selected a pile, he would say, "You sell some, you bring me some money. Ok?" We took him some of our shekeres to

---

1 East Coast Lesbian Festival, a women's music festival in New York.

get his advice. He bought a bunch, then he ordered some more. I said, "Hold on, you are actually buying shekeres from us?"

After that, we started to make deals with other craftspeople who did not want to travel to festivals. We got a larger booth to accommodate rain sticks, drums, rattles, toys, t-shirts, and so forth, and we started The Rainbow Guild and shared the booth with Womyn of Color who could not come up with the festival fee. If their craft was successful and they made money, they could apply for a booth of their own at subsequent festivals. Amoja started writing whimsical flyers about the booth. I would get off from my festival job [at Michigan] each day and go around taping up these flyers in the Portajanes, and they would disappear. We were dejected, until we found out that wimmin liked the flyers so much they were harvesting them to take home.

We became obsessed with wanting Sweet Honey in the Rock to see our shekeres. Then it happened—we were doing an outdoor festival. We saw Aisha Kahlil walking toward our booth. She spotted us, rushed forward, came within a few feet, jaw dropped, eyes widened. She turned and left. A few minutes later the little booth was filled with Sweet Honey playing everything we had. The shekeres were never happier, and I was euphoric, to put it mildly. Aisha Kahlil ordered one. Bernice Johnson Reagon ordered one with yellow wooden beads. It was the first one we ever made with wooden beads. Those shekeres appeared with Sweet Honey on the cover of a national magazine.

We continued making shekeres. By now we were living in a 170-year-old log cabin in Virginia and buying gourds from a widow woman in Wrens, Georgia. The woman in Georgia had long rows and rows of skids piled with gourds. We would get to her farm, put on coveralls, and scramble through the piles. When gourds dry the skin turns moldy, stinky, and flakes off. Add bird droppings to the mix, and it was quite an adventure. Underneath all of that mess there were some gourds that were flawless. That's what we were looking for. I fashioned tools to clean out gourds. We wanted them to have a voice, to resonate when the player struck the open bottom. We found a high test woven rather than filament fish line. It was more flexible.

We got dipper gourds that we made into rattles and *guiros*, Latin American percussion instruments that produce a grinding sound when a stick is rubbed along notches on a gourd. We made small feminist neck wallets, herbal talismen, and designed t-shirts that Snake & Snake printed. We made cotton mice stuffed with homegrown catnip for cat toys. We also began fundraising for the Maat Dompin land project (see *Sinister Wisdom* 98, Fall 2015, 150–56) and designed t-shirts and Spirit Dolls for this.

Market Wimmin spent over 200 days a year on the road, and used the time in between to make craft items in our Virginia cabin. We tried our hands at a line of spicy seasonings—Mountain Mama Seasonings—buying assorted bags of ground spices that we blended ourselves and designed labels for the shaker jars. We bought beads for the shakeres from warehouses in New York, 20,000 plastic beads of each color, and stuffed them onto the beams in the cabin. We stored the gourds in camp hammocks which we hung from the ceiling.

Then, in 1991, while we were on the road doing the festival circuit, our cabin in Virginia burned to the ground, and we lost everything. When word of this got out, women from everywhere donated so generously toward our recovery that we went straight into the process of fundraising for Maat Dompim—the phoenix that arose from the ashes of Market Wimmin.

LESBIAN THEATRE

Merril Mushroom

Theatre is performance art. It can take place indoors or out, in a wide variety of settings, with or without formal sets, and can involve one or more participants. Theatre can be serious or humorous, dense or clear, scripted or spontaneous, planned or extemporaneous. Lesbian theater, specifically by, for, and about lesbians, often was political in nature as well as being entertaining.

Lesbians in theatre might be writers, actors, directors, musicians, or multimedia artists. They could be poets, playwrights, songwriters, dancers, set designers, stagehands, puppeteers. They might perform as individuals or with others, with or without audience participation. Some lesbians perform their own material and some perform the work of others.

The stories that follow, condensed from much longer interviews, are of lesbians who have pioneered lesbian-feminist theatre in the South from the early 1970s until the end of the century. Most of the individuals interviewed have engaged with theatre as their primary form of creative expression through spoken word, mime, dance, music. Through their craft, these women both explored and expressed their lesbianism and their feminism in a wide variety of ways, and often performed at benefits for feminist causes. The one thing that most of these players have in common is that they have received little, if any, financial compensation for their work.

PAGODA PLAYHOUSE: THE GLORY DAYS
Merril Mushroom

The Pagoda, a lesbian community in St. Augustine, Florida, was established in 1977 as an arts and spirituality-oriented center by four lesbians who had a dream. A general herstory of The Pagoda appears in *Sinister Wisdom* #98,[1] and interviews with several residents are archived in the Sallie Bingham Center for Women's History and Culture at Duke University. This piece focuses on the Pagoda Playhouse, which was the cultural center of the community from 1977 to about 1997.

Morgana MacVicar, one of the founding mothers, was a dancer. She was an especially talented belly dancer and taught classes. Her students learned that belly dancing is a woman's dance—a dance of birth, a dance of our power. She worked at Distaff House in Tallahassee, Florida, until she lost her job because she was a lesbian. Later she moved to St. Augustine to be with her friend Rena, who was a singer/dancer/actress, and Rena's partner Kathy (KC). There she met Suzy, and they became lovers. They formed a theatre group called Terpsichore (the muse of dance) and performed throughout Florida. Their goal was to someday have their own theatre space.

One day Suzy saw an ad in the newspaper: "beachfront cottage for sale." They went to look at what turned out to be four cottages that were part of a larger vacation fishing complex called The Pagoda. The women bought the four cottages and leased the main building. At first they lived on the second floor of the main building. On the ground floor was a three-car garage and workroom that the women gutted in order to create their theatre.

As Rena Carney describes this process:

---

1 Merril Mushroom, "Pagoda – Temple of Love," *Sinister Wisdom* 98 (Fall 2015): 53–61.

They built a 20' long by 12' deep raised stage, set up a backstage bar which opened to the pool, and purchased fifty folding chairs from a local church which was closing. Can lights (vegetable cans from a local school) were built, and two frennels were hung, with the control panel at the back of the house near the right rear garage door. Suzy went to the theatre supply house in Jacksonville for yellow, pink, and lavender colored gels for the lights. A massive sound system purchased from JUICY (Judy Miller's lesbian band which had gone out of business) was set up. The dressing room was the old tool room behind the stage. They had a long board set up as a dressing table with mirrors and lights for putting on makeup. Costumes were hung on a clothesline. The hot water heater was in the stage right upstage corner, but no one cared.[2]

Photo courtesy of Rena Carney

Rena Carney as Goddess of the Moon, entering through the purple vagina, in rehearsal for a *MoonWomb* performance at the Pagoda Playhouse, 1977.

---

2   From a draft of an unpublished personal memoir, "The Pagoda, Pagoda Temple of Love, Pagoda by the Sea, 1975-2014: Rena Carney – Notes, personal and various sources," used with the author's permission.

One of the first sets was a backdrop that KC had made for Terpsichore performances—a big, purple vagina. It had a split that performers could enter and exit through. KC glued actual pubic hair along the labia, which she cut herself from the mons of friends who came to a pubic hair donating party. According to Rena, "The pubic hair was painted, so it was sort of surreal."

Rena and Morgana performed many times at that theater. In November 1977, they opened with a dance performance to Meg Christian recording of Sue Fink and Joelyn Grippo's song "Leaping Lesbians." Artists, musicians, and other performers were invited to show there in exchange for a week's free stay in the cottages. Flash Silvermoon was one of the first to perform there, and the Berkeley Women's Music Collective owned a cottage for a time and gave one of the first concerts. In addition to art and music, the Playhouse sponsored lectures, discussion groups, and other events. In a newsletter story from 1988, Pagoda resident Marilyn Murphy gives a long list of events at the Pagoda:

. . . concerts by Barbara Ester, Alix Dobkin, June Millington; two art exhibits: sculpture by Myriam Fougere and a mixed media show, "Junk, Funk, and Xerox" by Sarah Carawan and Rainbow Sue Williams; Ffiona Morgan's talk about her "Daughters of the Moon" Tarot; four meetings on anti-semitism, racism, and class. A forum on the issue of safe space for battered Lesbians. Circles for full moon, equinox, candlemas, whenever the spirit moves one; Lesbian movies/video night and umpteen veggie potlucks to celebrate almost anything at all.[3]

Over the years, as lesbians visited the Pagoda or joined the community, the playhouse remained as a vital cultural and political center.

---

3 Published in the Los Angeles *Lesbian News* under Marilyn Murphy's by-line as "Letter from Florida," dated April 3, 1988.

Brooke Triplette (left) and Dore Rotundo as ugly step-sisters, flanking Emily Greene as Prince Charming, *Princess Cinderella*, 1980.

Pagoda Playhouse performance of *Princess Cinderella*. In this curtain call, characters have turned into Amazons (l to r): Joanna, Rena Carney, Morgana MacVicar, 1980. (Emily Greene, as Prince Charming, is behind Morgana.)

ALL THE WORLD'S A STAGE

Gail Reeder

I didn't really mean to get into theatre, but it was the only non-nerdy afterschool activity an army brat could join without a local birth certificate. I never made cheerleader. I didn't know the right girls, and besides, I couldn't do flips. I went to four high schools and five colleges. Wherever I was living, I always found friends backstage.

I was a junior in high school in 1963, when racism was wrenched out of the darkness where it had simmered for 150 years in the small Southern town where I was living. I became active in the movement for racial equality and voting rights. From marching in sympathy with Selma, I progressed to the antiwar movement and participated in SDS (Students for a Democratic Society) doing visual pieces at demonstrations. Burning baby dolls with napalm soon led to feminist consciousness-raising, and I was out there burning bras with the best of them. It was another form of theater, but I don't think I recognized it at the time.

I became more and more active in the antiwar movement and joined an underground newspaper collective, *The Quicksilver Times* in Washington, DC. We were on the far left, somewhere between Mao and the Weather Underground, fighting as Che would say, "In the belly of the beast." Bringing down the establishment didn't leave much time for theatre, but I read about collective theatre troops in China that traveled from village to village, passing out red books and entertaining the farmers with tales of the revolution fought against painted backdrops by firelight. Guerilla theatre. A new tool for the revolution was born. I wanted to join those traveling troops. I wasn't particularly into bloodshed, but I did want to close the curtain on capitalism.

One of my assignments at *Quicksilver* took me to cover a guerilla-style theatre troupe appearing in a DC park. Earth Onion was a local group of women under the direction of Judith Z. Miller. They were dressed in military drag and presented a clever piece showing Nixon with the puppet dictator of Vietnam on his knee. It was funny and educational and spoke to my theatre-starved heart. I wanted to work with them, but my collective felt I would better serve the revolution remaining chained to my typewriter. I was shamed into political correctness and stayed with my IBM Selectric, but I am sure Earth Onion would have been more fun.

In 1974 in my travels after the collective collapsed, I was visiting somewhere in West Virginia in a wooden shack with an outhouse when chance brought me in contact with a woman who told tales of a theatre company that was both outraged and outrageous: Red Dyke Theatre in far off Atlanta. I saw but a glimmer of them through her eyes, but I wanted to see more. I wanted to be where they were. I wanted to become one of them. When a job opportunity opened in Atlanta, I readily moved. To my great disappointment, their demise coincided with my 1978 arrival. The women were still around, but like old lovers, they just weren't together anymore. I got to see Pici do her outstanding stand-up and hear Jaen Black in Moral Hazard, an all-women band. Later I saw a video of a Red Dyke performance, but it was like watching an old black-and-white movie. The images flickered and the sound was bad. I had missed them.

Fortunately, Atlanta was a city with many stages. I found myself doing *Blue Heaven* by Jane Chambers with Denise Haskins in a gay men's leather bar. That was an educational experience to be sure. They got to see two dykes living in the country with a goat in the kitchen, and I got to see my first "glory hole."

Also in the bar scene, I remember Nancy Oswald appearing with a penis puppet the size of an oven mitt doing a routine she called Dick and Dyke. It was clever and political.

Another woman's theatre group caught my eye, The Sisters of No Mercy. They weren't all lesbian, but at least they were feminist and into fighting classism and racism. They sang old union songs and voiced Holly Near rebellion. Leslie Friedman ran the group with a tight fist. I might never have gotten in except they needed a woman to play a man in a piece, and none of them was butch enough to handle it. Actually, Maria Dolan, the one lesbian member, was butch enough to handle it, but she was already playing the other male part, the chauvinist pig who was the villain of the piece.

The Sisters sometimes appeared at fundraisers and in demonstrations on the steps of the capital. Dressed in Sunday best, we billed ourselves SLAW (Southern Ladies Against Women). We sang songs and carried signs with white gloved hands. Soon Maria and I were writing for the group and the Sisters started doing some lesbian pieces along with the rest of their political pieces.

Leslie and I took video courses through the Public Broadcasting System. The result was the film *The Amazon Broadcasting System*, which the group wrote, taped, edited, and acted in together. It depicted an evening of irreverent programing where anchorwomen kissed goodnight after the national news, and Dykes in Space explored "where no man has gone before." Both political and ribald, it received lots of laughter and good reviews at the San Francisco Gay Film Festival in 1985. After that high point, the group took a different direction, and we parted ways.

The training in the use of video equipment came in handy when I got involved in taping a lesbian soap opera about a women's music festival. *Oh Goddess!* was the brainchild of Gwen Moore, and it was one of those skits that morphed into six episodes of amusing interaction. The best thing about the sessions was I got to know Deb Calabria, who had theatre aspirations of her own.

Deb began holding comedy workshops at SAME (Southeastern Arts Media Education), a queer, creative coalition run by Rebecca Ransom. Five of us, three women and two men, formed the core of an improv comedy troupe. We had already bought our SAME t-shirts and booked our first gig when Rebecca stepped in and demanded to know exactly what we planned to do. She wanted a script to see if we would represent SAME in proper fashion. We explained that it was improv and we never knew what we would be doing or saying until the audience offered suggestions. Rebecca pulled the plug on our association. Thus another group, Funny that Way, was born out of necessity, and we never looked back.

Funny That Way was sexually mixed, racially diverse, and multi-generational, but it was Deb Calabria who drove it, so I always saw it as feminist and gay. Most of the guys in the group liked to wear dresses, so we considered them one of the girls anyway. We focused mostly on queer politics and fun. Deb thumbed her nose at political correctness. That did not always sit well with me, but I feel in general we meant well. We were reaching larger audiences. What began in the bars soon was appearing at colleges and a music festival, and finally at the National Lesbian Conference, held in Atlanta in 1991.

We began to do real plays written by Deb and Mark Cox with higher production values. But it was never a collective. Like most theatre situations, there was always a director who controlled from the top. My efforts at contributing ideas met with heavy resistance, and more than once I was thrown out of the group. Sometimes I think they kept me around because I made all the costumes.

Funny That Way continued entertaining and educating until 2002. After that I think I had finally had enough. I knew I would never find the theatrical collective of my dreams. I had acted with groups that I like to think made a difference and helped get others involved in changing society.

Now I do a different kind of theater. Some of it is more recognizable, like stand-up comedy, but I also do English country dancing with a lesbian, gay, and transgender group called Quicksilver. Men and women dancing outside of traditional roles make for unexpected visuals and questions role definitions.

Sometimes theatre is merely costume. Last gay pride parade I marched in an OLOC (Old Lesbians Organized for Change) t-shirt that read "This is what an old lesbian looks like." Audience response was favorable. I high-fived so many people that my arm was sore the next day.

Now I am playing with slam poetry. It is amazing to hear so many people stand up and speak from their hearts on any number of once forbidden subjects. It is a more solitary theatre scene, but it is theatre all the same. Soliloquies for social justice. They may not see it as guerilla theatre, but I do.

Photo by Gail Reeder

The Sisters of No Mercy, 1982, laughing all the way. Top (l to r): Darlene Carra, María Helena Dolan, Lesly Hirvi Fredman, Middle (l to r): Eleanor Brownfield, Noël Augliere, Jesse Merle Harris. Bottom (l to r): Jeanne Shorthouse, Lee Heuermann, Gail Reeder.

RED DYKE THEATRE

Merril Mushroom

Frances Pici and Mickey Alberts have been in a long-term relationship, although they are not lovers. When they were in college in Buffalo, NY, in the 1970s, they created Stars and Dykes Forever Theatre, which grew out of their feminist activism and awareness of the invisibility inflicted on lesbians by the straight feminists in the movement. They wanted to bring lesbians out of the closet through theater, but also wanted to challenge the restrictions that were being placed on the presentation of the lesbian-feminist. Mickey was getting a lot of flack because of her "femmie" choices in her appearance. She says, "Butch and femme were okay for the working class community, it appeared, because that was their roots, but we (university students) were not supposed to engage in that. We were supposed to be androgynous, and anything else was supporting the patriarchy."[1] She got fed up with that attitude and joined Pici in Atlanta, where Pici had moved both to hide her lesbianism from her family and to enjoy the Southern women.

They lived in a communal household called Tacky Towers, a group of women who all were involved with theater, dancing and boogying, and lesbian/feminist politics, and became active in ALFA.[2] They continued to challenge the attitudes of the time about butch–femme, penetration, and sexuality/sensuality. Pici says, "I think Mickey and I were driven by not wanting to be censored. There is a value in exploring things that are taboo. It expands your

---

1 Quotations for Mickey Alberts and Frances Pici are from Rose Norman and Gail Reeder's interview with them, at the home of Gail Reeder, Atlanta, GA, June 28, 2015.

2 ALFA is Atlanta Lesbian Feminist Alliance. See Charlene Ball, "ALFA: Intersections, Activism, Legacies 1972-1994," *Sinister Wisdom*, 93 (Summer 2014): 58–66.

mind. You can refine it. If you're working in a box, you can't really go outside of the box regardless of where the box is placed."

At that time in Atlanta, there were four gay men's bars that had drag shows, two lesbian bars that did not have shows, and a mixed bar. "Red Dyke Theatre was a response to our lesbian sisters who wanted theatre that was not male-identified," Pici explains. "All . . . performances were benefits for the gay community, the women's bars, ALFA, the softball teams, or any issue that was a legal fight." They began by doing lip-synching to popular music, impersonating the female impersonators and lesbianizing the names of the groups, like Gladys Peach and the Clits, Peach Midler and the Dykettes, Dykeanna Ross and the Superbs, and the like.

Excerpts from their mission statement explain what they were up to:

> We use the technique of drag, yet we are not trying to be drag queens. We are women portraying women in non-stereotyped ways. Our appearances and styles are varied as yours and each as important to RDT as you are to the community. We are struggling to shake off the negative self-image of women created by magazines like *Playboy*, the media, and the society in general. We are trying to get in touch with our bodies and to see sensuality as one of life's primary joys.

> Creating a new culture within the old is a difficult task, and we are forced to make compromises. The music we use is not strictly by, for, or about women. Most of it is; however, the music coming from another oppressed culture. RDT feels a solidarity with the struggles of all oppressed groups, whether they be gay, third world, or poor.[3]

---

3   In the June 28, 2015, interview, Mickey Alberts read aloud this mission statement from a program for a performance called "Red Dyke Theatre Presents: Another Staged Climax," dated March 19, 1977, Metropolitan Community Church, Atlanta.

Red Dyke Theatre was a stable group. The core members were the group from Tacky Towers—Pici, Mickey, Jeanne Aland, Murry (Mary) Stevens, and C.C. Later in 1975, they were joined by Jaen Black, Fanny F., Donna P., Harriett Green, Bonnie Netherton, Wilson H., Dino M., and Sarah H. Sue B. and C.K. were the sound crew, using Sue's nakamichi tape deck and the group-owned reel-to-reel. Debra Gray did the lighting with equipment that was largely rented or borrowed.

Photo courtesy of Frances Pici

Members of Red Dyke Theatre, late summer 1975, in the back yard of Tacky Towers (l to r): top row, Phanny F., Donna P., Mickey Alberts; middle row, Murry Stevens (in Pici's arms), Frances Pici (holding Murry), C.K., and C.C.; bottom row, Jeanne Aland, Jaen Black.

Mickey: We always had someone be a stage manager. Toward the end, we decided we needed a director for each show. For a while it was very egalitarian. Nobody was in charge. It's amazing how it all happened. . . . We wrote things collectively. We had overnighters, brainstorming. . . . The process was communal, and there were really no leaders, because even the director was not a leader, just someone with more responsibility.

Pici: Because we all came from a living collective, our model of creativity was that everybody had a voice, everybody had equal time, to some degree, on the stage. . . . At the same time, we were meeting the needs of our audience who wanted to see certain skits again. One thing we did that the audience embraced was that the women audience members would come up on the stage while we were performing and stuff money or notes down our dresses, or come up and just give us a kiss. This was a ritual that happened and still happens in the gay clubs. [The lesbian-feminist activist Charlotte Bunch came to see a show, certain she would not like it because of this, but instead] was so thrilled at how that dynamic unfolded. To her, it represented women coming out of the closet, presenting themselves on the stage, being physical with another woman in a public venue. . . . Our shows were interactive. There wasn't a strong dividing line between the audience and the stage.

In late 1978, the choice had come down to keeping their paycheck jobs or continuing with Red Dyke Theatre. Coming out as lesbians in the earlier part of the decade, the women knew, as Pici says, "that we were going to have to support ourselves. In that environment, there was no chance that . . . any male financial support would come our way. . . . A job was . . . the key to any independence we had created in choosing to be who we were as lesbians." The idea of corporate sponsorship was totally against the group's politics. The shows were not for profit, and so the group disbanded. Pici continued working as a solo act doing mime until 1984. She went to work for CNN and then Emory University. Mickey worked for the State of Georgia until her retirement in 2009.

GAINESVILLE'S LESBIAN VARIETY SHOW: NOT JUST ANOTHER TALENT CONTEST

Barbara Esrig

It was never assumed that vigorous high spirits was antithetical to good works. For about twenty-five years, the Lesbian Variety Show was an annual ritual in the Gainesville, FL, lesbian community. I interviewed Beckie Dale, Amber Waters, and Patti Carnuccio to hear about how it got started and how it evolved.[1]

Beckie: The Variety Show started in 1987 or 1988, and Ky Gress was the force that made it happen, as a way for the lesbian community to come together in fun and entertainment. She found the place for the first two shows, the Acrosstown Theatre on South Main Street, and had some ideas, along with Woody Blue. Woody got a script for something called Dyke Trek, a take- off of Star Trek. We were making fun of ourselves, with skits and music and no particular talent, but coming together as a group and creating a performance.

And women paid money to see it! The whole other goal was a community fundraiser. Each year, any profit we made was given to honor either an individual or an organization in our community. After the second year we had outgrown Acrosstown. We tried several places, but the city's Thelma Bolton Center was absolutely the best for us.

Another goal was wide participation. We recognized really early on that if we encouraged a lot of different womyn from different groups in the community, they would encourage their friends to come so that everybody could feel a part of it. For the first Variety Show, we created flyers and talked to everyone, and they showed up. We contacted the Lavender Menace [softball team] audience.

---

1 Barbara Esrig interviewed Patti Carnuccio and Amber Waters on November 23, 2015, and Beckie Dale on November 24, 2015. All quotations are from these interviews.

Wild Iris Books helped advertise and sold tickets, and every year someone took flyers to the bars.

We encouraged all our friends, everybody, to perform. There was a core group of four to ten of us who would start coming together about five weeks early. We spread the word that we were having an organizational meeting about skits and that everyone who wanted to come should bring ideas and things they wanted to do. And they'd get their friends together to do it. I remember one year, a loosely connected friendship group from a Twelve Step program did a take-off skit of a Twelve Step Astrological Program. It was silliness, making fun of ourselves and how we can be in the world. Some of the skits were take-offs of popular TV shows like *Jeopardy*. They twisted it into questions about lesbians in the community. They called *The L Word* the *L Herd*. It was just very fun.

There was always a manager, Ky at first, and later Madeline Davidson, who got in touch with different groups that were going to do acts and helped them figure out what props they would need. At show time, she would get women on and off the stage smoothly. Almost every year there was a new emcee, and often she herself was entertaining, telling jokes during set changes.

Costs went up, but the price of the tickets remained a sliding scale from $1 to $20. As time went on, it cost more and we had to rent chairs and mikes. For a while there were refreshments we tried to sell. Then we started having a craft show. We did things to bring in different parts of the community besides those on stage. Some ideas were successful and some not so much.

Amber: The first Variety Show I went to was in 1990 or 1991. It was a reflection of the community of women who wanted to have a place to do their thing without men being involved, without that iconic male energy.

Whenever Patti and I were creating something for the Variety Show, we would have really good energy. Skits evolve in the moment with what's going on. Like when we did the skit about

Lesbian Bed Death or How Glucosamine Saved the Lesbians from Bed Death. That was totally inspired by real events.

Most of the songs we chose for the Variety Show were Patti's favorites. She's more comfortable dancing than singing, so she wanted to pick something she liked to dance to. She loved the Bee Gees tune "Staying Alive" [so we changed the title to] "Gainesville Dykes," and then we sat down and started writing the song. It was often just the two of us, but Denise Burnsed or Kathy McGlone may have been a part of writing that song with us. At first we were just thinking . . . who were the Gainesville dykes? And that's why we had about ten verses—it was just too much. We had to cut a lot of it. Denise was usually the one we recorded because she was comfortable singing. McGlone and I both sang in the original "Gainesville Dykes" crew. This song/skit was performed so many times.

My favorite skit was "If Hillary Were President." The premise was that all the men in the country would have to register their penises as lethal weapons and have them tattooed with a registration number. So all the women playing men, like a frat boy or a telephone lineman or a businessman, they all had to come to this very bored social worker who was so put out having to do this with her degree, look at men's penises and record them and how horrifying that was!

Patti: My first experience at the Variety Show I felt empowered. When I first went in, it was scary. I'd look over my shoulder because my experience in gay bars was real different. There were some old diesel dykes standing around outside to walk you to your car because otherwise people would hurt you, so why would it be any different here?

But it felt right. Somebody told me about the Variety Show, and shortly after that I began to perform. "Wake up Little Suzie" was the first song I did. I wanted it to be unique to us, to fit the whole community. I didn't want to use their words. It was about getting caught, you and your girlfriend. You fell asleep and your father or your husband was on the phone saying, "Wake up little Suzy." I always liked to work collaboratively with other dykes, even [on something] as simple as a song.

Photo courtesy of Pat Paul

Diana Slut (Pat Paul at right) and the Super Supremes (Dotty Faibsy on left) singing "Stop in the Name of Love."

Beckie: Why did it stop? Well, I think it kind of ran its course. I think it was a really amazing event that had its own life, and there was a lot of silliness and creativity and a kind of trust within the broader community. We could laugh at ourselves and with each other. That was the best. The planning of it and the time spent developing skits and coming up with ideas was probably the most fun part of it. Being on the stage was the culmination, but the five weeks leading up to it when you were with the same people over and over again was the fun part and helped expand or create the key sense of community that kept it going.

Amber: I think it ended for the same reason [the softball team] Lavender Menace ended. Women coming of age had a whole different means of expressing themselves and reaching out to each other. And all the young women didn't see themselves as lesbians. They didn't like that title. "I'm not a lesbian, I'm queer or I'm a boi." Someone said to me that *lesbian* was such an old-fashioned word. And I asked, "like *milkmaid*?" We've been categorized with the milkmaids of the world. Oh my god! The word *lesbian* has become archaic!!

Patti: I tried to keep it going, but it just wasn't happening. It wasn't that I failed. It is just too easy now to be gay. You can go out, go dancing anytime. It just isn't needed anymore. We evolved. The Variety Show had a wonderful life. It helped us become what we are, legally as well as culturally. It kept us united, politically active and out, and people could see that we're OK.

SPIN THE SPIRAL: HEALING INCEST

Phyllis Free

> *"What symbolism, if any, this rigid form concealed,*
> *has been lost."*
> ~ Encyclopedia Britannica *(circa 1984)*

Spin the Spiral: Healing Incest is a performance piece that is part of a larger multidisciplinary body of work, the Sestina Project. It all began in the late 1970s, when I participated in a small writer's group with other Atlanta writers, including Alice Teeter and Elizabeth Knowlton, who were also among the earliest participants of Womonwrites, the first gathering of which I attended in 1979. We met regularly around the big dining table of the communal lesbian household commonly referred to as "the Teeter House," where I lived as a tenant at the time. In addition to gaining support from each other by sharing our work and our process as writers, we also spent time studying and learning about various conventional poetry forms. I credit Elizabeth Knowlton for my first introduction to the complex ordered form of poetry known as the "sestina," which eventually led me into an unexpected, long-term journey of interdisciplinary exploration and artistic creativity, self-named "The Sestina Project."

The sestina is a complex, ordered form of poetry, the origin of which is attributed to a twelfth-century Provencal troubadour named Arnaud Daniel. The original form consists of six sestets (six-line stanzas), followed by one three-line envoi (tercet), often referred to as the *tornado.* In a specifically prescribed order, the end-words of each of the six lines of the first stanza are rotated throughout the poem as end-words for the lines of each successive sestet, followed by the placement of prescribed pairs of end-words in each line of the closing tercet, with one at the end of each line, in specified order. While numerous variations of this form have been adapted by poets throughout the centuries (e.g., creating double or triple sestinas, using variations in meter, etc.), the prescribed rotation of end-words remains as the most consistently identifying factor in distinguishing this form.

The evolution of my "Sestina Project" began in Hilton Head Island, in the fall of 1983, when I completed a poem called "Autumn Sestina," inspired by Knowlton's poetic example and using the "form" (i.e., abcdef, faebdc, etc.) as a guide. Upon completion of the poem, I became obsessively intrigued by the structure of the form itself, wondering if and how it would be possible to determine the prescribed rotation of the end-words of the first six lines through the five successive stanzas (sestets) and the final three-line stanza (tercet) without the "form" to use as a guide.

This guiding question compelled me to embark upon a journey of artistic exploration to discover how and why the sestina form was structured as it was. I began by charting the rotation of the end-words in the form of visual graphs of geometric and curvilinear configurations. This process revealed a series of visual images which, after months and months of "graphic analysis," eventually led me to the conclusion that the primal symbolic image which serves as the root and source of the sestina structure itself is the archetypal image of the spiral. This discovery led to a period of independent study and research, during which I delved into the pervasive and recurrent use of images, such as those appearing in my graphs, as archetypal symbols in various world cultures, as evidenced in contemporary, as well as ancient, cultural, and spiritual artifacts and rituals.

As more and more visual images appeared during the course of my "graphic analysis," my mind became flooded with visions of how these images might be expressed and interpreted through visual artworks, music, creative movement, and dance. As this work-on-paper (and in my imagination) continued to evolve, I began to envision a staged, interpretive performance piece based on the images revealed in my exploratory graphs and drawings.

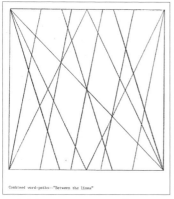

Courtesy of Phyllis Free

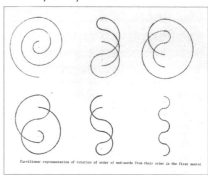

(L) Fig. 1: "Between the Lines": is a combined image of linear graphs representing the consistent rotation of each end-word from one line to another through the six sestets.
(R) Fig. 2: Curvilinear graphs represent the line placement of each end-word as it moves from one stanza to another through the six sestets.

I began to share my excitement and interest in exploring this concept of "interdisciplinary translation" in conversations with anyone who would listen, especially with other feminist artists whose conceptual grasp of the scope and possibilities of this work further fueled my desire to manifest such visions. Artist-mentor Abby Drue's validation of my identity as an "artist," and her response to this work as a "significant" and "long-term body of work," along with her advice and encouragement to find other artists as collaborators with whom to share my vision, was a critical spark in lighting a fire that still glows with hot embers, casting visions of new works, even to this very day.

After moving to Louisville, KY, in 1990, I was encouraged by artist Debra Clem and author Martha Barnette to apply for a grant from the Kentucky Foundation for Women for funds to bring my vision of a performance piece to life. Recalling earlier conversations with Atlanta harpist/composer Susan Ottzen, who had expressed interest in composing music for the imagined piece, I invited her to apply as my co-collaborator. With my visions and various graphic interpretations of the sestina structure as inspiration for the overall production design—expressed non-textually through interpretive music, choreography (see Fig.2), scenic elements, and installations (see Fig. 1)—and Susan's interest in using this structure as a narrative vehicle for sharing the story of her recovery as an incest survivor, we received a grant to develop and produce *Spin the Spiral: Healing Incest*.

This production was presented in Louisville by Artswatch in the MeX Theatre at the Kentucky Center for the Performing Arts and in Atlanta by The Georgia Council on Child Abuse at Seven Stages Performing Arts Center. In addition to facilitated post-performance discussions of the production concept and narrative after each show, local therapists were engaged to provide emotional support for audience members, as needed, in response to the content of the production. Video documentation was provided by DeKalb Prime Cable, and a copy of this video was subsequently used in classes at Oglethorpe University as an example to demonstrate how the arts can be used as a powerful tool to address sensitive social issues such as incest and family violence.

DURHAM'S LESBIAN THESBIAN: DALE WOLF
Merril Mushroom

D ale Wolf is a playwright, mime, performer, educator, and veteran of the North Carolina arts community. Born in Manhattan and educated at Temple University, where she majored in Communications and Theatre (BA 1976), Dale moved to Durham, NC, in 1976. She has studied mime with several professionals and founded Touch Mime Theatre. Founding members of Touch met in Tallahassee and the company was formed in Carrboro, NC, in 1976-77. She has written and performed such pieces as *In the OUTfield* and *50! Evolution of a Butch Lesbian*. She also produced and appeared in an award-winning local children's television program, *Barney's Army*. She co-founded with Dorie Drachman and others the Triangle area theatre company Lesbian Thesbians (1990–91), which produced and performed plays by and about lesbians. She currently and for many years has worked with gay youth organizations.

Lesbian Thesbians was a theatre company in the Triangle area (Durham–Raleigh–Chapel Hill) of North Carolina. In their September 1991 program, they describe themselves like this:

> Lesbian Thesbians is first and foremost a creative avenue for the community at large to see lesbians and find out that we are a vital and spirited part of our community. We're also an outlet for lesbian actors to perform as lesbians, playing lesbian roles, and for lesbian playwrights, whose plays are not often performed, to reach a wider audience. Finally we provide an arena where lesbians can be creative about the lives they know best, their own.

In 1992, she premiered her monologue *In the OUTfield*.

Dale: *In the OUTfield* derived from my personal narrative of coming out in the South. I did it because Jesse Helms won [his 1990 Senate race], and I was mad. I just wanted to put a face out there and see what happened. It was terrifying, of course, to put myself out there like that. In fact, I got a letter from a high school teacher in Raleigh asking me not to step out on that stage. I still have that letter, very voluminous, with an outline of all the quotes from the Bible telling me why I shouldn't be talking about my "agenda," whatever that was. But I did it, and did it many times, touring it to really great feedback. What's really valuable to me now going back and looking at the materials I saved are the handwritten letters people wrote in response to that. That's what made it art. If I could communicate something that touched someone in that deep a way, that to me was art.

Dale Wolf, publicity shot for *In the OUTfield,* 1990.

Dale's show *50! Evolution of a Butch Lesbian* deals with issues like aging, abortion, drugs, George Bush, and our health system. Another piece "was about my father's death while in hospice care. I'm really proud of this piece. I combine text with mimetic movement and dialogue with my dad. It was a beautiful moment of mime. . . . There's really something special about being with someone while they're dying. I had reconciled with my father after not having spoken to him for many years."

Paul Whetstone wrote all of the music to go with Dale Wolf's lyrics for *In the OUTfield* and for *50! Evolution of a Butch Lesbian.* This is from *In the OUTfield.*

Crush Song

> I had a crush on the girl next door.
> She never noticed.
> We were friends, nothing more.
>
> I had a crush on the girl next door.
> I'd see her in the halls at school.
> My heart would just soar.
> I'd gaze at her at lunch time
> Then I'd look through the floor
> Cause I had a crush on the girl next door.
>
> We'd sit up real late at night
> Talk til around four.
> I gave her a flower once.
> She asked, "What's it for?"
>
> I had a crush on the girl next door.
> She never noticed.
> We were friends, nothing more.

JACQUI SINGLETON:
SINGER, SONGWRITER, PLAYWRIGHT

Merril Mushroom

Jacqui Singleton was a Virginia singer, songwriter, playwright, director, and lesbian activist. She wrote her first play when she was a senior in high school in Norfolk (although she said in a YouTube interview that she used to write dirty stories when she was in grade school). She said, "My creative writing teacher had me write a scene, and it turned into a play which she got produced on public TV in Norfolk.

By the time she graduated in 1977 from Longwood College as a theatre major, she had written thirteen more one-act plays. In 1979, she performed at the first Pride event in Richmond. She played the guitar and sang with The Richmond Jazz Ladies but also performed by herself and put together bands that played at festivals. In 1984 she founded Artists Alliance, a theatre group under the wing of the Richmond Department of Recreation & Parks. Her play *Crazy Man* was produced by Off-Off Broadway in New York in 1982, but it didn't come to Richmond until 1994. Jacqui thought it would be unsuitable for Richmond because it had a lesbian relationship in it.

During that time, women were not represented very well in theatre, and Jacqui was instrumental in bringing women's stories to the forefront. Mary Isemann, who met her in the Longwood theatre department, said of her, "She had a tendency to cast shows with her heart. She had a vision for her shows and might cast somebody that nobody else agreed with. She was an original. She knew what she wanted, and it always worked."[1]

In 1992, she helped start Richmond Triangle Players. She was on their board and directed her own play *Manny & Jake* as their first

---

1 Jacqui Singleton's obituary in the *Richmond Times-Dispatch*, March 4, 2014, www.richmond.com.

full-length production. She produced and directed plays written by herself, Carolyn Gage, and others through her production company JERA Entertainment, Inc. She staged a play she wrote, *Journey Home*, which told the story of her discovery of the white owners of her mother's family in the antebellum South. She also headed Singleton Entertainment LLC, an artist development and music event business.

Jacqui wrote several published novels (including two adult fantasies featuring a lesbian heroine) and a children's story. She died in 2013 at the age of fifty-eight from complications of several physical illnesses.

Photo by Bobbi Weinstock

Jacqui Singleton (with guitar at right) and her band performing for Richmond Lesbian Feminists New Year's Eve party on the eve of 2000. [Originally published in *Lesbian and Gay Richmond*, by Beth Marschak and Alex Lorch (Charleston, SC: Arcadia Publishing, 2008), p. 113.]

VIRGINIA ARTIST PATRICIA R.CORBETT
Merril Mushroom

Patricia Corbett is an award-winning playwright, advocate, artist, educator, published author, and feminist entrepreneur whose passions are community service, social justice, and education. She just completed an MFA in Interdisciplinary Arts from Goddard College, Plainfield, VT. Patricia encourages marginalized populations to seek their truth, claim their power, and tell their stories. Her father, Linwood Corbett, Sr., was a community organizer, civil rights activist, and minister who greatly influenced her life and her work. He sent his entire family to college working as a baggage foreman for Greyhound bus line and custodian at Virginia Union University where she earned her Bachelor of Arts degree in English. At some point in his early life, her father shared with her that he had wanted to be an actor. Patricia's mother, Mary V. Corbett, is a poet and artist as well as a retired educational professional and the first Black professional clown in the state of Virginia. The combination of these two extraordinary parents supported Patricia's passion for community service, social justice, radical disorientation, writing, and humor.

Patricia always considered herself a writer of poetry and short fiction until, on a whim, she turned one of her short stories, "Fall of the House of Snow," into a play. As a result, she received a Maryland State Arts Council Individual Artist Award for Playwriting. The play tells the story of how a group of men and a devoted woman become family as a result of their rejection from their families, communities, and churches. Set in the late 1980s against the backdrop of the rapid rise of the HIV/AIDS epidemic, "it was a story that had to be told,"[1] Corbett goes on: "Nothing had been written about the psychological and emotional impact this had on families

---

1 All quotations are from Rose Norman's phone interview with Patricia Corbett, December 2, 2015.

in the black community. I thought a creative approach would bring some humor and lighten some of the heavy issues in *Fall of the House of Snow*, such as discussions about HIV/AIDS, the church, homophobia, violence within the Black community toward gay people, particularly transgender people, and how to reconcile with internalized homophobia." *Fall of the House of Snow* is one of three major projects currently in progress.

Aunt Maggie's Mojo or The Devil in Angel Brown is a novel that Patricia is immersed in as well. This historical fiction tells the story of three generations of Black women who are clairvoyant. The story starts in Southeastern Africa in the early 1700s, moves to Virginia in the early 1800s, North and South Carolina in the early 1900s and ends in the 1980s back in Virginia. One of the main characters is a lesbian detective who has a strange affinity and connection to the case. The novel explores familial ties, secrets, and the metaphysical.

Patricia's one-woman show, tentatively titled *Nobody's Darling*, is based on a poem of the same title by Alice Walker. The spirit of Audre Lorde is the inspiration for the six characters in the play: a seventeen-year-old Black woman who was the first to be executed in the state of Virginia; Black Transgender Warrior Barbie, an FTM transgender doll fictionally created by Mattel, who engages the audience to vote on whether this transgender doll should exist. Then there's an African warrior, a poet, a washed up 60s poet, and Harriet Jacobs, a slave who ran away and hid in the attic space of a house for seven years. All of these are truly powerful stories. I'm very much interested in using art to elevate all kinds of causes and all the issues we tackle from a feminist perspective.

A small experimental theater in Richmond is interested in working with her on *Nobody's Darling*, and she hopes to get started next year.

Toward the end of the twentieth century, Patricia started JUSTaSISTA Productions, providing writing, editing, and personal historian services. JUSTaSISTA's mission is ". . . to educate, enlighten, as well as provide a space for the storytelling of marginalized populations . . . to shift paradigms in business, education, and the community." She also founded Sisters Rising Mentoring Organization for girls: "We started by just providing a space for them to talk about what was happening in their lives. That evolved to helping them set up bank accounts, applying for college, all kinds of interventions in terms of social services they needed and other kinds of guidance." Unfortunately, Sisters Rising folded once Patricia left Virginia twelve years ago, but she has returned to Virginia, and she hopes to expand this programming into Sisters Rising Academy, "a boarding school for inner city girls, with the hope of developing an entire community dedicated to supporting young women . . . in self-actualization and independence."

"As an artist," concludes Patricia, "one of the most difficult things in being a Black lesbian, and a mother, and all the other things I am,

Photo courtesy of Patricia Corbett

is not the creation of my work. It is creating it through the process of living everyday life in a society that constantly devalues women and Black people. As we look at what's happened in our past and in our current society, none of us have room to suppress our stories anymore."

Virginia playwright Patricia Corbett.

FEMINISM DANCES OVER WALLS OF TRADITION
Kathleen "Corky" Culver

With fun-filled fervor, second-wave feminists dived right in and evolved every aspect of dancing, turning rigidly heterosexist models that privileged men into dances that empowered and freed women.

Dancing Both Lead and Follow

Social and ballroom dance classes were a virtual barricade where patriarchal custom gave women a mandatory subservient role. They would begin, "Okay, men line up over here to learn lead parts. Women, you will learn follow." The theory was that women need men's leadership. (This in an actual world when back leading was about the only way to get anything moving.) In the St. Petersburg/Gulfport, FL, area, Phyllis Plotnick, a dance teacher, led a ballroom dance revolution. She gave classes in which women could learn both the lead and follow parts so they could dance together and experience both parts. Phyllis' classes in the 1990s created a large dance community. The first dances they held were brave events in a time when being seen in same-sex dance couples could result in lost jobs, families broken apart, and violence. At first they put black paper over the windows, so they could have a sense of safety and privacy for their, of course, "gay" waltzes and swings and salsas. The black paper over the windows has long since come down. In fact the Sonia Plotnick Health Fund rented the St. Petersburg Coliseum or the elegant Casino dance hall for the annual Valentines Ladies in Red dances, well advertised and attended by thousands.

Lesbian dances provided women opportunities to court, to see how two could negotiate precision and playfulness, find good fits and good times, wondrous energizing of connection. On the grand scale, the gatherings developed communities with social cohesiveness, pride, and physical and mental health. Not that outrageous a claim, as dance has been proven to double the benefits of ordinary exercise in terms of Alzheimer's prevention, since it engages both right and left brains, listening, cooperating, memory building, quite an array of joyful skills, a wonderful sense of agency.

Photo courtesy of Phyllis Plotnick

Phyllis Plotnick teaching the large Gulfport, FL, lesbian dance community Melissa Etheridge's Stroll, 1996, when the windows were covered with black paper.

Belly Dance Revolution

Feminists who researched belly dance discovered its true ancient origins. It was created, not for enticement of men but as preparation for childbirth, for women's spiritual heritage of being in harmony with nature, with connections to undulating rhythms and circles of the cosmos, not performed in bars, and not performed for the male gaze as objects. They left off the marketplace look, the coins in the costume that implied they could be bought or controlled by money. They eschewed the nearly nude look and reincorporated forceful and martial moves that declared independence. The transformative power of these dances was felt by performer and audience. Morgana MacVicar's privately published pamphlet *The Matriarchal Art of Belly Dancing: A Feminist Perspective* and her own dancing embody the strength, spirituality, and drama of this consciously feminist Goddess dancing.

Photo courtesy of Emily Greene

Morgana MacVicar dancing on the beach behind The Pagoda, about 1978.

Modern Dance

Isadora Duncan, of course, freed dance and dance philosophy, advocating natural motion and dress. This philosophy was taken up eagerly by lesbian dancers and Southerners for whom comfortable, loose fitting, light layers were cool and liberating. The constrained and racist enslavement of both owners and slaves were opened to fearless self-expression never before seen. Also exploring new forms of movement, Sarah Salamander Thorsen does Sacred Dance. For years, she has trained and taught dances in honor of Tara, the female Buddha (see taradancesangha.org). Tara's twenty-one aspects have provided opportunities for self-choreographed dances as well. In 1995, Sarah was initiated as a priestess in the Mystery School. She performed these dances at Womonwrites, the Meditation Center, and the Pagoda. Like Isadora Duncan's, these were spiritual dances, and very beautiful.

Photo courtesy of Gail Reeder

Sarah Salamander strikes a pose at Womonwrites, 1990s. Feminist-inspired dance shows women as strong, with agency and grace.

DANCING WITH SYLVIA "SYCAMORE" TOFFEL

Rose Norman

In 1976, Sylvia "Sycamore" Toffel filmed a segment of the *Today Show* (later an article in *Life Magazine*), performing with a Black male dancer, Tim Reed. Inter-racial dancing was an unusual and dangerous thing to do in Toffel's hometown of Birmingham, AL, at that time, but her mother's dance studio there had always been integrated. As racially volatile a city as Birmingham had been (known as "Bombingham" in the 1960s), the dance school experienced very little racial pushback. "Once or twice when we were performing, there were incidents," Toffel says.[1] "Once at Avondale Park in Birmingham, while we were dancing some people threw rocks at us. We got off the stage quickly. Then in 1978 at Tarrant High School in Birmingham, Tim and I performed a duet, and they told us we couldn't do that duet in the second show." Resisting racism was only one way that Sylvia Toffel practiced lesbian-feminist activism in a lifetime as a professional dancer and movement educator.

Born in Chicago, she spent her early childhood in San Juan, Puerto Rico, and has lived most of her life in Alabama, where her mother, Laura Toffel Knox, was artistic director of ballet companies in Montgomery and Birmingham. In 1967, Knox started Birmingham Creative Dance (later Southern Danceworks), the company in which Toffel danced professionally for many years. She began studying dance at age seven and continued in ballet and modern dance, improvisation, movement education, and then into contact improvisation. For a year, she performed with Ram Island Dance Co., in Portland, Maine. From 1978 to 2010 she taught creative movement to elementary school students as an Artist-In-Education in Dance with the Alabama State Council on

---

1 All quotations are from Rose Norman's interviews with Sylvia Toffel in Huntsville, AL, on June 9 and December 11, 2015, and April 11, 2016.

the Arts. She also performed and taught workshops at the Southern Women's Music & Comedy Festival in Georgia (1987 and 1988) and at Rhythm Fest (1990–94).

Photo by Janice Hathaway

A publicity photo of Sylvia Toffel from the late 1970s.

While she was determinedly out from the age of seventeen, Toffel was thirty-five years old before she created her first dance with a lesbian-feminist message, a dance to Holly Near's "Emma," celebrating Emma Goldman. Before that, she had danced a piece called "Couple," originally choreographed by male choreographers for two men.[2] She had seen it and been so impressed that she

---

2 "Couple" choreographers were Stephen Koester and Terry Creach.

asked the choreographers to arrange it for her and Lyn Buchanan, another member of Southern Danceworks, but she did not see that as making a political statement:

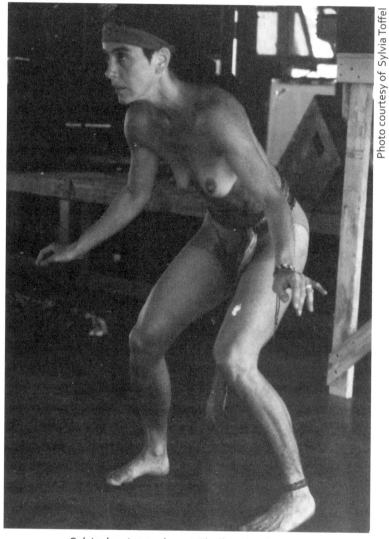

Photo courtesy of Sylvia Toffel

Sylvia dancing topless at Rhythm Fest in1991.

I remember when we performed that in Greenville, AL, I heard people saying "Was that a lesbian dance?" That was really curious to me, because all I saw was two women dancing together. We were lovers, but I didn't relate it to that. It's what other people bring to it. It's a really beautiful dance. I could see where people might say that because we're very intimate with each other, lifting each other, rubbing each other, but it was choreographed like that. It was contemporary dance in the finest of duets that I have ever done.

In 1993, she began choreographing a dance using the words and the image of the American Modernist author Gertrude Stein, performed with a larger than life puppet depicting Stein through a two-sided painting, young and old. The title *So Come Along* is from the end of Stein's book *The Making of Americans* (1925). Toffel dances to a recording of Stein reading "Family Living" (also from *The Making of Americans*), as well as music by Stein's friend, the composer Virgil Thomson. "It started off as a solo, with Gertrude the puppet sitting in a rocking chair," Toffel says. "I was thinking of Gertrude as a lesbian icon." The segment begins with Toffel reciting a passage from *The Making of Americans*, beginning "She is queer and will interest you." In the closing segment, she changes to gym clothes and dances to "Ode to a Gym Teacher," by Meg Christian, a contemporary lesbian icon.

Toffel performed this piece as a solo in 1993 at a Southern Danceworks production at the Carver Theatre in Birmingham, and again in a Women Working performance in Asheville, NC. In 1994, she moved from Birmingham to Huntsville, AL, and began working with puppeteer Anna Sue Courtney. Toffel asked Courtney to join her in the duet, holding the Gertrude mask and adding movement to the performance. Toffel always dressed as Alice B. Toklas in both the solo and the duet, but says that "I kind of folded between them [Gertrude and Alice]. I never felt like I was one or the other." The dance is "an abstract rendition of what Gertrude Stein was writing about."

For Toffel, dancing and lesbian-feminism were two different tracks in her life, tracks that crossed mainly when she began attending and performing at women's music festivals in the 1980s. "To be able to dance at those festivals was exhilarating," Toffel says. "That was a rare opportunity to dance for a lesbian audience, that and Pride events in Birmingham and occasional events by Magnolia Productions, a lesbian collective that brought women's music to Birmingham." Yet even those festival experiences did not bring the two together. She still thinks of herself as a lesbian who is a dancer, rather than a "lesbian dancer."

Photo courtesy of Sylvia Toffel

Sylvia with "old" Gertrude puppet
(puppet worn by Anna Sue Courtney, painted by Art Price), 1995.

SOCIAL DANCING

Merril Mushroom

When I was coming out as a bar dyke in South Florida in the 1950s and 1960s, ballroom dancing was all the rage. It was a wonderful means of socialization, seduction, and showing off. We danced in the gay bars, on the pavilion of the gay beach, and at private parties. Good dancers could be popular for that attribute alone, even with nothing else to recommend them.

Ballroom dancing was the style of partnered dance taught by studios like Arthur Murray (indeed, lesbians and gay men often were employed as Arthur Murray instructors). It was done to "easy listening" music—mostly pop and jazz. In the bars or on the beach, we danced to 45 rpm records played on a jukebox, six plays for a quarter. In private homes, we danced to vinyl records played on a Victrola. We danced to Johnny Mathis, Dinah Washington, Ella Fitzgerald, Etta James, The Platters. We danced to all the old rock and roll and rhythm and blues singers, Tito Puente, Bunny Berrigan, and Edith Piaf. There was a whole group of folks at the Alton Road bars who had learned authentic, actual, French dance to "Milord" and taught it to others. We danced many versions of foxtrot and two-step (which we called "slow dance" and included waltz) and Latin, which was very popular among us South Florida folks: mostly cha-cha-cha, but also mambo, rumba, samba, pasadoble, and some tango. We fast danced to rock and roll, doing varieties of lindy, panama city, chicken, bop. We did line dances like the madison and that famous outgrowth of the madison—the hully-gully and we did sexy dancing like the fish and the dirty boogie.

Dances had "steps"— a particular pattern of moving one's feet that was done in time to the music for traversing the dance floor (e.g., forward and side step, back and side step, walk, walk, and side step). We could get written instructions with printed footprints to follow in learning the steps. Once one grasped the basic pattern of steps, one could improvise, move in any direction at any rate of speed and in any configuration, using big steps or small, in a limited area or sweeping around the dance floor. There was an infinite number of possible patterns of dancing that a pair could engage in, usually face to face, but also side to side, or face, side, or back to back, close together or separating. We might break into fancy dancing, doing floor dips, side dips, hesitations, syncopations, twirls, turns, lifts, changing handholds. Steps and moves coalesced into a unified event with the music and rhythm, limited only by the creativity of the dancers' imaginations and the space available.

Social dancing was a good way to make new friends or find lovers. Standing face to face and touching each other, we could engage in conversation during the dance while really checking out how our bodies fit. Usually we would dance together in same-sex pairs, but we crossed genders for an especially good dancing partner. We also always had to keep alert for any hint or warning of plainclothes police who lurked the beach and the bars looking for perverts to arrest. When they were around, we would pair off to dance heteronormatively, but who was leading and who was following was not always clear-cut.

Ah, yes, leading and following. This skill has fallen into disuse as ballroom dancing has fallen out of fashion. Sometime in the 1970s, it seemed that people stopped touching each other when they danced, stopped leading and following but moved separately, independently, dancing alone as an individual instead of moving with a partner like one unified organism. Within the parameters of the dance, leading and following can change and flow among the partners, or they can remain static, or they can change with partners or over time. The leader holds her partner so that their bodies touch along the lengths of trunk and limbs, and where they meet, they merge in awareness of the contact. Feeling the music, the beat, the leader transforms these into movement—of breath, muscle, joint, energy. The follower relaxes, gives up all control, allows her partner to bring her along into that pattern of motion. She doesn't so much move with her partner as she allows herself to be moved with her partner by her partner.

Phyllis and Cheryl 1996. Phyllis dancing lead here. "Sometimes we switch follow and lead in the same dance," Corky Culver says. "Lesbian egalitarianism."

Even in dances where there is less body contact, less touching, more active movement, more "steps," the signals come to the follower from the leader through places where they do touch—hands, arms—communicated through a moment of full body contact followed by a push of hips, shoulders, hands, and, most important, the psychic connection, the nonverbal link that is forged between the partners by sensing the music and the beat and submerging awareness into the paired experience.

Some people were strong leaders, easy to follow and trustworthy. Some were great followers, never pulled against the lead or got too floppy to move themselves. Some could do both at will, and some were not very good dancers at all in any way. But there always was a place for anyone who wanted to come to the dance floor with another person and move about, body to body, while the music played.

WOMEN'S MUSIC FESTIVALS IN THE SOUTH
Barbara Ester

Ten years after the dawn of Women's Music Festivals, Robin Tyler, producer of the West Coast Women's Music & Comedy Festival, took on the Deep South. She was warned that it could be dangerous and that "it's never been done."[1] She went ahead anyway, renting Camp Coleman in the Georgia mountains, and starting the Southern Women's Music & Comedy Festival (SWMCF) in May 1984. With name performers, great sound, cabins, lakes for recreation, crafts area, workshops, and other appealing amenities, the ground was secured. Robin felt "there was a lot of initial resistance to our coming down there." There was a lack of trust the first year. The Californians came across as arrogant and patronizing to some of the Southern festival workers. But after a bumpy start, Robin considered that "we have successfully integrated."[2] Well-known women's music circuit performers from the South like Meg Christian and Teresa Trull were right at home at Southern, along with other local performers. There were a few complaints about the terrain and accessibility. Writing in 1990 for *Hot Wire*, Jorjet Harper called Southern a "live and let live festival" and found it "less politically charged" than other festivals she had attended.[3] Compared to other festivals, "Southern was more like a lesbian vacation,"[4] with night stage held in a roofed theater with real chairs for the audience! As far as explicit lesbian visibility, Harper (who is from Chicago) found Southern to be "one of the more radical," in that "Lesbians of diverse subcultures seemed to

---

1 Toni L. Armstrong, "The P.T. Barnum of Women's Music and Culture: Robin Tyler" (Interview), *Hot Wire*, 4.2 (March 1988): 5.

2 *Ibid*.

3 Jorjet Harper, "Southern: The Live and Let Live Festival," *Hot Wire*, 6.3 (September 1990): 40–41.

4 *Ibid*., p. 40

coexist quite well." Harper found that diversity did not extend to race: "Aside from the performers, there was a startlingly low proportion of women of color."[5] But 2000 festi-goers created a successful beginning, and Robin held onto Camp Coleman for eight years. She struggled with the politics of the camp's security in legal confrontations and had to leave Camp Coleman before folding in 1992.[6]

Yer Girlfriend playing day stage at SWMCF 1989.

Photo courtesy of Phyllis Free

Robin Tyler's challenges were nothing compared to what the Hensons faced in Mississippi,[7] but SWMCF inspired a new trend in the South. Brenda and Wanda Henson attended the Southern Festival, took what they experienced, and brought it on home to Mississippi! They were emotionally, intellectually, and spiritually inspired to create their own style of festival. Brenda writes that

---

5 *Ibid.*, p.42.

6 Robin Tyler moved the festival from north Georgia to its last site, in North Carolina, only to be confronted again by religious organizations.

7 On the Hensons and Camp Sister Spirit, see Marideth Sisco, "'A Saga of Lesbian Perseverance and Steadfast Resolve,'" *Sinister Wisdom* 98 (Fall 2015): 142–145.

Wanda "put the whole thing together in ninety days with thirty-three volunteers. Her spirit is catching."[8] There were 250 festi-goers at the first Gulf Coast Women's Festival in March, 1989, and Suzanne Pharr "opened the festival with a speech on 'The Southern Woman,' putting everyone in touch with her wonderful, rich, Southern culture and how important it is to celebrate our heritage."[9] Gulf Coast became a force of change for "sisters who had never seen or heard their culture [lesbian culture], whose lives were changed *forever* by the music and the sights!"[10] Keeping festival sites and what became Camp Sister Spirit safe was challenging for the Hensons. The festival's tone was all about community and spiritual enhancement. They acquired their own land for festivals, but as challenges intensified and national media got involved, attendance suffered. The festival was alive and well for fifteen years. Camp Sister Spirit also hosted Spiritfest with a focus on woman-oriented spirituality.

Women in the South didn't have to wait long before another festival sprouted a "new attitude" on Lookout Mountain with cabins, lake, and all the usual festie requirements. Rhythm Fest was billed as the "new women's festival," and appeared on the scene in the fall of 1990. Produced by a cooperative and billed as a festival of "women's music, art and politics," the festival set a goal of operating without hierarchy among "organizers, workers, entertainers and festi-goers, who mingled quite easily and comfortably."[11] There was always a lineup of name performers and locals, like Yer Girlfriend and the Reel World String Band. Great music, good energy, and 1200 women gave Rhythm Fest a great start. Alive and well for six years and known as "a well organized

---

8 Brenda Henson, "The First Gulf Coast Women's Festival," *Hot Wire*, 6.1 (January 1990): 38.

9 *Ibid.*, p. 39.

10 *Ibid.*

11 Marcy J. Hochberg, "A New Attitude, a New Festival: Rhythm Fest 1990," *Hot Wire* 7.1 (January 1991): 38.

festival without an elitist attitude,"[12] Rhythm Fest ended in 1996 when negotiations for the camp broke down.[13]

Excitement and enthusiasm for festivals waxed and waned. The challenges to keep locations safe in the Bible Belt festered. Those three major music festivals in the South are now old memories. Other, smaller festivals dotted the Southern landscape and were advertised in Lesbian Connection, Hot Wire magazine, and national and local newsletters. Winter Womyn Music in Charlotte, NC, the Virginia Women's Music Festival, SisterSpace in Maryland, the Lesbian Bizarres in Miami, and Womenfest in Key West are a few examples. Another Southern Women's Festival ran in Florida and Georgia from 2000 to 2007, originally produced by Pat Cobb. Attendance of 200–2000 fluctuated, as did the location. Some festivals continued and new, smaller venues occasionally appeared.

Dedication and commitment to women's music and lesbian culture were changing. A new generation of lesbians became devotees of performers who were given better access to the various forms of public media. Many more lesbian performers were out and could be heard on radio and television, in mainstream concert venues, and on all kinds of techno-savvy media. But older lesbian generations passed down a legacy of doing it in the South in spite of the challenges. Womyn's lives were changed. Lesbian Connection still lists two pages full of "Regional Festivals and Gatherings," mostly Pride events, and only a few festivals nationwide. In the South, the Virginia Women's Music Festival continues in May. SisterSpace and Womenfest are held in September, and the Amazon Music Festival is in April in Fayetteville, AR.

---

12 Ginny Risk, "Rhythmfest [sic] 4," Hot Wire 10.1 (January 1994): 28.

13 A letter from Rhythm Fest producers to "Womyn in support of Rhythm Fest," dated May 28, 1996, details the series of negotiations that led to canceling Rhythm Fest 7. They had had to use four different campgrounds in the six years, and the search for a fifth campground ended when the second set of negotiations broke down in 1996. See Michelle Crone Papers (1927–2000), Albany, NY, M.E. Grenander Department of Special Collections and Archives. "Bulk date" 1982–1995.

TIMELINE:
WOMEN'S FESTIVALS IN THE SOUTHEAST

Barbara Ester and Rose Norman

Even though some of the festivals listed here were not entirely women's music festivals in the larger sense, they were community events that brought in women musicians and artists and fostered community-building. Some are outside our timeline, but are included because they are still going on, or (in the case of Southern) to distinguish them from festivals with a similar name.

1974 ~ **Women's Renaissance Festival**, Gainesville, FL. Organized by a group of Melrose lesbians known as Kampho Femnique Frothingslosh (KFS for short), the festival was held at the Thomas Center in downtown Gainesville and showcased women artists of all kinds—music, dance, fabric art, painting, drumming—plus workshops on skills for empowerment like oil change and small motor repair.

1974–76 ~ **Richmond Women's Festival**, a one-day women's festival, held each year in city parks in Richmond, VA, sponsored by the Richmond Women's Alliance, a coalition of women's organizations. Because these were held in public parks, men could not be excluded, but organizers promoted the festivals as women's events. In the 1980s, Richmond Lesbian Feminists (an organization that still exists today) began producing weekend women's festivals at a state park, and continued those annually until the Virginia Women's Music Festival became a regular event (see below).

1978–83 ~ **Women's Jazz Festival**, Kansas City, MO. Featuring jazz greats like Marion McPartland, Betty Carter, and Mary Lou Williams, this festival showcased jazz's most prominent women, but Margie Adam was in charge of open mike and encouraged others to get onstage and play. Original organizers were Carol Comer and Dianne Gregg.

1982–88 ~ **Sisterfire**, Takoma Park, MD, one of the few women's music festivals open to men. Sponsored by the arts organization Roadwork, executive director Amy Horowitz.

1984–92 ~ **Southern Women's Music & Comedy Festival**, produced by Robin Tyler at Camp Coleman in north Georgia, until 1992, when the last festival was held in the Blue Ridge mountains near Hendersonville, NC.

1984 and 1985 ~ **Lesbians for Empowerment, Action and Politics, LEAP**. Held over a long October weekend on women's land near Gainesville, FL, these festivals featured musical performances and jams, art displays and vendors, and an array of workshops from politics to spirituality, with 250 lesbians camping and collaborating.

1987 ~ **Winter Womyn Music I** ~ Charlotte, NC, produced by Retts Scauzillo.

1989–2003 ~ **Gulf Coast Womyn's Festival**, first in Gulfport, MS, and after 1993 in Ovett, MS, at Camp Sister Spirit; produced by Brenda and Wanda Henson.

1990–95 ~ **Rhythm Fest**, first held on women's land in northeast Georgia (1990–92), then on a succession of camps in Black Mountain, NC (1993), Swannanoa, NC (1994), and a camp near Aiken, SC (1995). Producers included Michelle Crone, Mandy Carter, Billie Herman, Kathleen Mahoney, and Barbara Savage.

1990–present ~ **Virginia Women's Music Festival**, first produced by Janet Grubbs Green in a field next to an old schoolhouse she owned in Goochland, VA, then at women's land called InTouch, which became CampOut when sold to another women's group. Since 1991, this festival has been held at that women-owned land halfway between Richmond and Charlottesville, VA. It continues to be held on Memorial Day weekend. http://www.campoutva.com/

1990–93 ~ **Lesbian Bizarre**, Miami, FL. Held at the lesbian restaurant, Something Special, the Bizarre had vendors, performers, massage, food, and impromptu music making.

Photo by Pat Paul

Flash Silvermoon and Corky Culver entertaining the leapsters, LEAP 1984.

1991–93 and 1999–2001 ~ **Spiritfest,** held in the early years at Fontainebleau State Park on the north side of Lake Pontchartrain, in Louisiana, produced by Brenda Henson, and in the later years at Camp Sister Spirit near Ovett, MS, produced by Ayla Heartsong.

1995 ~ **In Gaia's Lap: The Maryland Womyn's Gathering,** held over a weekend in May. Their *Lesbian Connection* ad reads "This circle of Allies is spiritual, social, political and transformative."[1]

1996 ~ **Heart of the South, Womyn's Dance and Music Extravaganza**, held over a weekend in June at a hotel in the French Quarter of New Orleans. The same organization also produced Heart of the West in Las Vegas for several years, but this appears to be the only one held in the South. Producers were Marina Hodgini and Maile Klein.

1998–present ~ **Womenfest Key West**, held in September, and billed as "the largest gathering of lesbians and friends in North America." http://www.womenfest.com/

1999–present ~ **SisterSpace**, started in the Pennsylvania Poconos in 1974; moved South to Maryland in 1999, and runs in September. http://www.sisterspace.org/

2000–07 ~ **Southern Women's Festival**, held in Florida and Georgia, produced by Pat Cobb.

2013–present ~ **Amazon Music Festival**, Fayetteville, AR, in April. http://www.bigbadgina.com/amazon-fest

---

1 *Lesbian Connection*, January/February 1995, p. 11.

GAINESVILLE
WOMEN'S RENAISSANCE FESTIVAL, 1974

Kathleen "Corky" Culver

In the 1970s, we had a group in Gainesville called Kampho Femnique Frothingslosh (KFS).[1] We were interested in music, art, and having a good time, and we wanted women artists to be recognized. Lorelei Esser was a major spark for this direction. First we staged a small women's arts festival in Jacksonville, and then a big Women's Renaissance Festival in Gainesville in 1974. The festival was to showcase women artists of all kinds—music, dance, fabric art, painting, drumming. The focus on women made it a breakthrough event in a time when women were given little attention. We had three tents and a large stage. We had workshops on changing your oil, small engine repair, and other skills for empowerment. We had sickle cell testing, workshops on quilting, dance troupes, quilt-makers, political action tables. There was a special tent for performing pelvic self-exams. We had only one speaker all day, Katura Carey, of the African Socialist Party. We wanted to show women's art and have people experience it; at that festival we were not into argument and accusation or victimhood, but celebrating what women actually have and are.

Held on the lovely Thomas Center grounds, a beautiful old Spanish hotel, the festival drew hundreds of people, some dressed up in capes and face makeup. "Lesbian was not foregrounded, but many women walked around holding hands. Some women said it was the first time they had ever seen such a thing. Many women still remember it as a life-changing event. Everywhere, without speeches, were eye-opening experiences of this new wave of feminism. A fantastic feminist theatre troupe, Feminist Guerilla Theatre, from near Tampa, did skits that blasted through

---

1 The silly name is explained in Corky Culver's "Sparks and Prairie Fires," *Sinister Wisdom* 93 (Summer 2014), p. 18.

old consciousness ("Smile," "Shaving"). Members of that theatre included Dee Graham, Kathy Freeperson, and Snake.

The festival was about freedom, and it was free. It was not at all about money—we were not trying to make any money. It was done out of love for each other and women's possibilities, opening up these things that had been suppressed, making women's arts unapologetically center stage.

Photo courtesy of Corky Culver

Abby Bogomolny (left) and Lorelei Esser performing at the Women's Renaissance Festival in Gainesville, FL, October 5, 1974.

ROBIN TYLER AND THE LIVE
AND LET LIVE SOUTHERN FESTIVAL

Rose Norman

For nine years (1984–92), the Canadian-born comic and lifelong activist Robin Tyler produced the Southern Women's Music & Comedy Festival (SWMCF), the third largest women's music festival in the country, after the Michigan Womyn's Music Festival (1976–2015), and Tyler's own West Coast Women's Music & Comedy Festival (1981–95, with gaps). Tyler came from a show business background, and attended her first women's music festival at Michfest in 1977, where her experience was that comics (and her onstage butch persona) were not welcome. That's what prompted her to produce her own festival in California, where she lives. What led her to start the Southern festival a few years later, though, was strictly political: "When I started the Southern festival, I didn't do it just to bring music and comedy to the South. I did it because I thought it would help the South organize."[1] As these special issues of *Sinister Wisdom* have demonstrated, Southern lesbian feminists had been organizing since 1968. SWMCF was like throwing a match on a wildfire, and they came in droves. They came for the music, yes, but more for the opportunity to network in lesbian community. Tyler brought major activists and organizers to speak that first year: Flo Kennedy, Kate Millet, Rita Mae Brown, and Sonia Johnson (when she was running for President). Those and other activists came again in subsequent years: Urvashi Vaid, Patricia Ireland (then NOW president), Sue Hyde (NGLTF director), Hilary Rosen (Human Rights Campaign Fund Co-Chair), and more.

---

1   Rose Norman interviewed Robin Tyler by phone on June 17, 2016. All quotations are from this interview. A substantive recent study of Tyler's career and her "charged humor" is by Rebecca Krefting, "Robin Tyler: Still 'Working the Crowd,'" chapter 5 (pp. 136–68), *All Joking Aside: American Humor and Its Discontents* (Baltimore: Johns Hopkins Press, 2014).

Lesbians in urban areas like Atlanta and Gainesville, FL, may have had more networking opportunities than those in rural areas, like activists Brenda and Wanda Henson in Gulfport, Mississippi. The Hensons attended SWMCF shortly after they first met in 1985. It was their first women's festival, their first experience of that kind of women's space. "This festival, Robin's festival, saved my life," Wanda Henson said in 1990.[2] "It was an immense amount of culture shock, but it was *my* culture, it was *my* people, it was *my* home. My whole life is different now. . . . No amount of therapy or anything could compare to the festival experience."[3] They immediately started a feminist bookstore in Gulfport (Southern Wild Sisters Unlimited, 1987–93), and started the Gulf Coast Women's Music Festival in 1989, moving it to women's land in 1993.[4] Robin Tyler helped them raise funds to buy that land.

Held over Memorial Day weekend, Southern drew a crowd of 2000 that first year and was held at Camp Coleman, in northeast Georgia, until 1992, when a new camp director led to relocating to a camp in North Carolina.[5] "Having 2000 lesbians in the woods in the middle of Klan country was challenging," Tyler recalls. "Everyone in the camp felt safe, but we had people patrolling the borders with weapons."[6] After the initial culture shock wore off, she found Southern women charming:

---

2 Quoted by Jorjet Harper, "Southern: The Live and Let Live Festival," *Hot Wire*, 6.3 (September 1990): 40–41

3 *Ibid*.

4 For the story of that women's land, see Marideth Sisco, "'A Saga of Lesbian Perseverance and Steadfast Resolve': The Hensons and Camp Sister Spirit," *Sinister Wisdom* 98 (2015): 142–45.

5 "The struggle to maintain the camp was enormous. I brought in the ACLU, NOW, etc., but because they [the camp] were a religious organization, we had no more rights than when The Boy Scout camp threw us out of Willits, California. (We had to move the California festival three times.) I do not think that people understand how hard it was, especially in the South, but in California also, to rent and retain land for lesbian festivals." Robin Tyler email to Rose Norman 12-27-16

6 Over the eight years at Camp Coleman, they only experienced one incident of men trying to enter the land, a group of drunks armed with a baseball bat.

Once they calmed down about us being there, everybody just fell in love (literally). . . . I found that Southerners were more like Canadians. They showed up on time. It was a fit. . . . The Southern festival was my *favorite* festival. They were more interested in the politics [than the women on the West Coast] and in the authors we brought. There was something to do every minute of every hour. Five things to do, or ten things. Also, there was a pool and a lake and cabins.

She also experienced the Southern women as not so "alternative" as what she had experienced at Michfest. By "alternative," Tyler does not allude to leather lifestyle or gender identity:

If people were into S/M or whatever they were into, that wasn't up to me. We were strict about drugs, but I didn't care about people's personal lives. Our fire captain at West Coast was a trans woman. . . . Rather than have the push–pull of who's a woman, who's not a woman, we didn't have a transgender policy. It was not problematic. And therefore, we did not split the festival over it. We as people want civil rights, and as lesbians we have been so oppressed. I think we have to set the example of not being scared (we're survivors, and we're tough), but also by not oppressing other people that are being murdered and mutilated all over the world. It never became an issue because I didn't make it an issue. . . . I wanted the focus to be on lesbian feminism.

Since the days when Southern drew 2000 women, women's music festivals are fewer and smaller. Tyler thinks part of that change is that the women who were attending those festivals in the 1980s and 1990s are now in their fifties and sixties, and more likely to be taking an Olivia cruise than doing something that requires camping. She also compares what happened to the women's music circuit to what happened to the African American "Chitlin' Circuit" of the 1930s—they broke through into the dominant culture, or some of them did:

Melissa Etheridge, the Indigo Girls, Tracy Chapman, Ellen DeGeneres, Lea DeLaria—they've all been accepted in the dominant culture, where there's more money to be made. That's the end of our own culture, the segregated culture. In a way it's sad, because you never get the feeling of safety we had in the Amazon cities of women that were festivals. There's nothing like it any more. . . . But it lasted a long time, from the 70s probably through the 90s. Even the antiwar folk circuit in the 70s did not last as long as the women's music circuit. When you finally break through to the general public, your own group loses that intimacy with you.

It's really sad that it's over. It was like creating a dream and stepping into it. I still have the energy to do it, to fight over the land. I did try to go back to Camp Coleman. I thought maybe we could do one last festival, all together again. I called last year, and they never returned my call.

Photo courtesy of Robin Tyler

The lake at the Southern Women's Music & Comedy Festival.

INTOUCH, CAMPOUT, AND
THE VIRGINIA WOMEN'S MUSIC FESTIVAL

Beth Marschak

Since the 1970s, various groups of Richmond, VA, women have organized and promoted women's music, from single concerts, to one-day festivals, to weekend-long women's festivals that continue to this day. In the 1970s, local women musicians played for a women's coffeehouse that met in different places at different times, including several churches. Over time, lesbians organized many concerts here, bringing Meg Christian, Cris Williamson, Alix Dobkin, and other well-known lesbian musicians. In the 1990s, Wanda Fears and I organized a number of lesbian music events, calling ourselves Purple Lady Productions. We would have a special night at various restaurants with a lesbian musician or group performing. The largest thing we did was a Lucy Blue Tremblay concert, beginning with a dinner for about a hundred people.

Photo courtesy of CampOut

CampOut logo. CampOut is a year-round women's camping and events location that hosts one of the few remaining womyn's music festivals in the South, the Virginia Women's Music Festival on Memorial Day weekends, as well as the Wild Western Women's Weekend over Labor Day weekends.

The women's festivals in Richmond in the 1970s were one-day outdoor events held in Richmond parks. The first was in 1974, at downtown Monroe Park, with Kay Gardner as our headliner. We held two more of these festivals, 1975 and 1976, always including music and workshops and other activities such as information tables.

In the 1980s and into the early 1990s, Richmond Lesbian Feminists (RLF) organized weekend-long lesbian-feminist festivals at Pocahontas State Park. Although they were specifically lesbian festivals, they were open to all women, as were most of the RLF events. These were not primarily music festivals, although they included music. There were workshops, swimming, boating, softball, arm wrestling competitions, lots of different things at those women's festival, as well as music.

The first Virginia Women's Music Festival was held in 1990, produced by Janet Grubbs Green on land next to an old schoolhouse in Goochland, VA.[1] That year, she and investors raised funds to buy women's land called InTouch, for the purpose of hosting the Virginia Women's Music Festival and for other women's outdoor activities. They sold enough shares to buy a hundred acres halfway between Richmond and Charlottesville, and began holding the Virginia Women's Music Festival there over Memorial Day weekend in 1991. InTouch ran all year-round, and people could come out any time they wanted for year-round camping, swimming, and canoeing in the seven-acre lake. InTouch organized women's outdoor concerts, and volunteers cleared land for the lake and built cabins, a stage, and a dance pavilion. The Virginia Women's Music Festival was their biggest annual event, followed by a country-western event, Wild Western Women's Weekend, held over Labor Day weekend. InTouch, Inc., all Richmond lesbians (many RLF members), later sold that land to another group of women, who re-named it CampOut. The Virginia Women's Music Festival grew from 75–100 attendees to about 300–500 festi-goers (at InTouch). CampOut continues to host that festival as well as the Wild Western Women's Weekend. Many

---

1 Rose Norman's July 15, 2016, telephone interview about InTouch with Janet Grubbs Green is archived at Duke along with other interviews from this special issue.

performers come from the region, including nationally known musicians like Tret Fure and Disappear Fear. Throughout the year, they have other events and rent cabins and tenting space for women. Owning the land has been important to the continuity of these Virginia festivals, plus they have an ongoing connection to the land throughout the year.

Photo courtesy of Janet Grubbs Green

"The Crew" building cabins at InTouch, early 1990s.

Photo courtesy of Janet Grubbs Green

The ropes course was a regular workshop at InTouch, early 1990s.

WOMEN'S MUSIC FESTIVALS AND LESBIAN FEMINIST PROCESS

Michelle Crone

As a worker at the Michigan Womyn's Music Festival in the 1970s, and later Robin Tyler's West Coast and Southern Women's Music & Comedy Festivals, and as a producer at Rhythm Fest, I was in charge of "Rumor Control." That was the name of a tent, and also a process for facilitating the resolution of issues people brought up. I had been trained as a grassroots organizer. Then, as part of an improvisational theater group in the West Indies, I learned to go with what is happening without questioning or judging. These skills helped me develop my lesbian feminist process that I have come to see as extremely revolutionary, then and now. We practiced and refined those processes at women's festivals.

I think self-esteem is vital to our growth as human beings, which then helps us interact with people as wholes, not just parts that we have had to show in order to survive. Festivals provided the space needed to allow this process to grow. We had every step along the way open to question, and indeed women did question. Individuals had to think deeply and defend why they were saying certain things, while as facilitators we would have to try to make the space as safe as possible.

This process was long hours and days in between building whatever it took to hold a festival for thousands of women. Whenever I would be running some of these sessions, I would rely on humor a great deal to soften or make points or release tensions. At times, I would ask for joint screams. Even now, after so many years, I find that the techniques are still as powerful when dealing with groups.

One of the main realities of feminist process was to make sure that diversity was there and that you were looking at all the things that held women down, such as classism and racism—all the "-isms". Because of all those "-isms," women's voices were pushed way down.

So for making an arena or environment where women could find their voice, and could voice whatever it was they wanted to voice, you often had to go through decades and decades of each woman's life of conditioning, depending on her cultural and family background. That's a *long* process, and a *slow* process. So when we would gather in circles to start processing around certain issues, often we would have to go through just hours and hours of women acting out, not knowing how to express what was going on, of making it OK and encouraging women to break that veil of silence that they had had to live with for so long.

Once that was done, once that started to evolve, once women started to get a taste of what it was like to say something that was not put down, it was an *amazing* process to witness. I'm not saying there was not conflict, or that women didn't disagree. We had some women who were so darned verbally dominant that we started having to come up with ways of not letting certain women take over circles, without using patriarchal rules like Robert's Rules of Order.

We always tried to go with consensus, but also use things like the talking stick, or passing the crystal, some kind of structure where women would have to share the stage for voicing, would have to not make it personal. You have to come from your heart, the I. You cannot blame.

That all came out of feminist process, and we carried that in with Rhythm Fest, and at the same time, we had to build a community in what were very often short periods of time. On some of the land, we had to put in electrical or pipe in water. At Cloudland (in northeast Georgia), we had women crawling under these very old outbuildings and fixing the plumbing. We had to bring in certain kinds of refrigeration in order to feed women.

But we had this experience from Michigan, building what we called the witches' kitchen, which was nothing. You know, we dug holes and put hay and ice and tubs for refrigeration. Or at Seneca Peace Encampment (summer 1983), we made outside kitchens and fire pits that were very functional. We had a lot of these skills that evolved from just needing to do it, and having women learn along the way.

I just wish that we could have captured that somehow, to continue to see it and feel it and smell it and breathe it, to see women evolve and become *empowered*. Hole-digging, ditch-digging, out-house building, you name it. Women at first thought, "I don't know if I can do that." And then, after a few attempts at it, they were ready to put on the tool belt and go out there and build a stage or whatever. It was an amazing, amazing process, and I know that wherever those women ended up in their lives, whatever path they created after these festivals, they got nourished from this process. They got self-confidence from this process. It made a huge difference in their lives.

Today, when I facilitate group process, I always make sure to give credit to the women of festivals when I am introducing techniques, especially when men are in the groups. When they are holding the talking stick, I want them to know that there is herstory here, and to honor the native tradition that we adopted to further our fair process.

RHYTHM FEST:
WOMEN'S MUSIC, ART & POLITICS (1990–95)

Rose Norman and Merril Mushroom

Susan LosCalzo of Lofty Notions, a craftswoman who worked the women's music festival circuit for two decades, was unhappy with the hierarchical structure of most of the festivals she attended. She found that some women got better food than others, some had preferential accommodations, some got better treatment. But Rhythm Fest was different. "That was the best festival I ever did," said Los Calzo, "because of the ethics. The festival . . . was very equal, and no one was going to eat better or worse than anyone else. . . . It was not classist in any way. It was egalitarian."[1]

Photo courtesy of Barbara Savage

Rhythm Fest producers (l to r) Kathleen Mahoney, Barbara Savage, Michelle Crone.

Rhythm Fest, the first of the music festivals in the South that actually included producers who lived in the South, was also the

---

1 Quoted from Robin Toler's phone interview with Susan LosCalzo on June 27, 2015. See also "Lofty Notions," this issue.

first to operate as a "workers' festival." Four of the producers—Barbara Savage, Kathleen Mahoney, Billie Herman, and Michelle Crone—met at Robin Tyler's West Coast Music & Comedy Festival. Most of them had worked at Tyler's Southern Music & Comedy Festival (the first festival in the South) and at the Michigan Womyn's Music Festival, and they all had ideas about how they wanted to do a festival that was different, more inclusive, more political.

Michelle had met Mandy Carter at the Seneca Women's Peace Encampment, and they had kept in touch over the years. Mandy had been a member of Real Women Productions, the group that produced women's music concerts in the Triangle area of North Carolina (1986–90). Michelle asked Mandy to join with them in putting on the festival, and after some hesitation, Mandy agreed.

Photo courtesy of Barbara Savage

Rhythm Fest producers Mandy Carter (left) and Barbara Savage.

The producers lived all over the country: Barbara in Tennessee, Mandy in North Carolina, Michelle Crone in New York, Kathleen and Billie in California, although Kathleen moved to Atlanta for six years while producing Rhythm Fest. One of Kathleen's best

Rhythm Fest memories is "when we would have our meetings throughout the year to get ready for the next one. I really loved those times with those women. It was very inspiring. It was just an amazing process to try to create an environment that was outside the box. It was incredible that we were able to do it with basically no money, no investors."

They each took on tasks they were good at. Mandy handled logistics—registration, volunteer work shifts, housing. Michelle and Kathleen did artist bookings. Michelle also facilitated all the meetings, and what was called "rumor control," while Kathleen was primarily in charge of the stage (she had managed Night Stage at Michigan). Barbara took care of all the food needs (kitchen and concessions). Billie did the books and finances. Of course, they all did many other things as well.

The name for the festival came from the back of an antique plate that Barbara had in her kitchen. It read "Rhythmware." Michelle and Kathleen were at Barbara's house in Tennessee, planning the festival. Barbara describes the scene: "Kathleen turned over the plate and said, 'Rhythm Fest.' We all said, 'that's it!' I remember that day."[2]

Rhythm Fest began on Labor Day weekend 1990 and continued for six Labor Day weekends before difficulties in finding a festival site forced it to end. The festival incorporated music, art, and politics. Social interactions around music and art, and working together to create an environment for festivals, ultimately leads to political action and is, itself, a form of activism. For example, one of the workshops at Rhythm Fest in 1990 was around organizing politically to try to defeat Senator Jesse Helms, the racist and homophobic North Carolina US senator who was running for re-election that year against Black democrat Harvey Gantt. Gantt was the first ever Black mayor of Charlotte, NC, and the first Black student to integrate Clemson University in South Carolina. Mandy was campaign manager for Senate Vote '90 that was supporting Harvey Gantt.

---

2 Quoted from Rose Norman's interview with Barbara Savage at Savage's Tennessee home on April 29, 2015.

Producer Billie Herman had been in law enforcement and later owned her own tax and accounting company. She initially headed Security at West Coast and Southern festivals, and she did not want to do Security any more. Keeping order and enforcing policies designed for safety did not make for popularity, especially as a woman of color in a position of authority in the South. She said, ". . . many, many, many of the white women attending Southern [festival] had no idea how to handle that. There were comments made. So it wasn't always fun for me."[3] She joined the Rhythm Fest organizers as a co-producer, keeping the books and handling the money. When Mandy Carter left in 1993, Billie took over some of Mandy's official duties.

A lot of the skills for living on land and accommodating over 2000[4] women had been learned through experiences at other festivals, especially Michfest, and the Seneca Peace Encampment.[5] Women came and worked, and they learned by doing.

Michelle: At Rhythm we had the bottom-line policy that we won't say no. We will say how can we make it work, and sometimes we couldn't. We tried, and sometimes we discovered it just wasn't going to work. But our mantra was "don't say no," and that was pretty major.[6]

The first workers at Rhythm Fest were people who had been kicked out of Michigan, Southern, and other festivals, usually because of festival politics and power dynamics.

---

3 Quoted from Rose Norman's phone interview with Billie Herman, November 9, 2015. All quotations are from this interview.

4 Attendance data are not readily available, but *Hot Wire* says the first Rhythm Fest drew 1200 women (January 1991, p. 59), and Kathleen Mahoney recalls that one year they drew over 3000.

5 Begun in the summer of 1983 in Romulus, Seneca County, New York, this women's peace encampment continued from July 4 through Labor Day. Women continued to have peace actions on that land until 1994, when it became Women's Peace Land.

6 Quoted from Rose Norman's phone interviews with Michelle Crone on May 18, 2015, June 3, 2015, and May 8, 2016. All quotations are from these interviews.

Michelle: For example, S/M women were frowned upon at Michigan. There was a real divide between the women who ran Michigan as a business and many of the workers, who were very grassroots and radical. I believe it was 1978 when Michigan changed from a collective to a cooperative and formed the LUNTS (Land Union Negotiating Team) and the CUNTS (Coordinator Union Negotiating Team). When Michigan started losing money, the CUNTS [which Michelle was part of] came forth and asked the workers not to be paid in order to save the festival. We also started collecting money toward buying festival land. We thought if we raised 15–20% of the cost of the land, then 15–20% of the land should be women's land, not going to the business. We raised thousands and thousands of dollars, and then it became really clear that the festival would bite the dust if some money didn't get raised. We were asked to turn over that money [raised for land purchase]. We held meetings, and finally reached consensus to turn over that amount, and when we did that, we were all asked to leave, fired. At subsequent festivals, when people were asked where we were, they would be told they couldn't talk about it because we weren't there to defend ourselves. That felt like character assassination to us. That's a big part of why we decided to start our own festival.

There were so many workers that Rhythm Fest was sometimes called "The Workers Festival," and the festival organizers deliberately intended for the workers to be empowered.

Michelle: Festie-goers were only there for three or four days, so they were not so much into the process. They were there to have a vacation or a good time, the community building, the joint feelings. It was the workers who were there for weeks at a time, building a vision. They were much more emotionally involved in how things operated, how women were being treated, their ideas being fed and nourished. They were there to help *create* something, not only to participate in workshops and listen to wonderful music. They were much more involved in nation building, tribal building.

At Rhythm Fest, we would break down the kind of hierarchical structure that some festivals had. We weren't afraid to talk about controversy if there was an issue on the land. We'd set up times and places to have dialogue about that. Rhythm Fest was committed to diversity, to freedom of voicing, to making it a safe place. . . . We didn't want to create any barriers, such as the areas at Michfest where you had to have a certain wristband, places like workers' or performers' eating areas. There would be Security at those areas of Michfest. We wanted everyone to have access to all areas. At some festivals, workers and festies would get certain food. Craftswomen would sometimes be denied food. At Rhythm Fest, everybody ate the same food. You would always be able to go up and talk to performers or workers. There would be no final decisions without discussions, and we always tried to reach agreements by consensus.

Mandy: We knew that other women's festival producers had, you know, wristbands, VIP areas, and so on. We weren't going to do any of that. We wanted to have a different culture, not like other festivals. We didn't want to act like we had more power than anyone else. . . . We booked acts that normally would not get into festivals.[7]

Kathleen: At that time, we were much more on the fringe [than other festivals]. Tribe 8 performed, Super Punk, some Goth bands, the more cutting edge, super political, outrageous bands. They didn't perform at any of the other festivals then, because they weren't asked to, though later

---

7 Quoted from Rose Norman's phone interview with Mandy Carter on March 24, 2015. All quotations are from this interview.

they did. We definitely booked more radical entertainers, like Lea DeLaria, who hadn't done many other festivals.[8]

Rhythm Fest also had festival favorites like Holly Near, as well as big-name performers like Melissa Etheridge, Emily Salyers, and Ani DiFranco, who were not regulars on the festival circuit. Melissa Etheridge actually worked on getting ready for that first Rhythm Fest.

Rhythm Fest was very popular with performers.

Kathleen Mahoney: After the first festival, the reputation really rippled out to the artist community about what a great environment it was. It was really easy for me to book entertainment. People just felt inspired by our desire to create a different type of environment, a more cooperative work environment. Everybody was treated the same. Nobody got a fancy anything. They came. They camped if they were able to. It was just a different process. People were intrigued and inspired by it. Performers were camping if they could. We had only a couple of cabins. Mostly everybody camped. There was no separation between workers, festies, producers, performers. During fest, everybody played together.

Although there was not a great deal of money, Billie felt that what there was was handled well. The producers were committed to making sure all the workers got paid and that women were reimbursed for their expenses. Rhythm Fest also made a commitment to profit sharing.[9] Michelle Crone says, "We never really made much of a profit. We never lost money, but there wasn't much profit to share, and usually what was left was spent on storage units, equipment, and other things needed. When there was profit to be shared, it was shared." For all the time the

---

8 Quoted from Rose Norman's phone interview with Kathleen Mahoney on May 13, 2016. All quotations are from this interview.

9 *Southern Voice*, September 27, 1990, p. 4.

producers put into planning and running the festival, they might take home $1000 each.

But Rhythm Fest was never about the money. The most important thing was how it felt to be there.

Kathleen: There's a magic that happens when you get onto the land, and you're immersed in nature, and you're immersed in this group of women that you only get to see once a year, and work side by side with them, building this amazing environment for women to come and settle into for an out-of-the-ordinary experience. I think that was the most fulfilling thing about it, when we were all (the workers) setting everything up, creating that environment, and then watching and being able to see all the people come and pay their money to be there, and settle into it, and be just so fulfilled. It was such a beautiful, *inspiring*, powerful, energy there. A lot of very spiritual women were there. Energetically, it absolutely vibrated through the whole festival.

Backstage at Rhythm Fest.

A LIFE OF POETRY, SOCIAL ACTIVISM, AND A "UNIQUE, PRIVATE" LOVE: AN INTERVIEW WITH NAOMI REPLANSKY

Sandra Tarlin

Photo courtesy of Naomi Replansky

Naomi Replansky, 1941.

Naomi Replansky is a self-taught poet. As a teenager, her work appeared in noteworthy literary publications: She was published in *Poetry Magazine* in 1934, and in *Contemporary American Women Poets: An Anthology of Verse by 1311 Living Writers*, edited by Tooni Gordi in 1936. One of the poems published in *Contemporary American Women Poets*, "You with the Roses," is a lesbian love poem which she wrote when she was fifteen. Among the poets in the anthology are Babette Deutsch, Marianne Moore, and Muriel Rukeyser.

Replansky was nominated for the National Book Award for her first book, *Ring Song* (1952). She has published a chapbook, *Twenty-One Poems Old and New (1988); and The Dangerous World: New and Selected Poems (1994).* Her *Collected Poems (2012),* won the Poetry Society of America's 2013 William Carlos Williams Award and the following year, Replansky was a finalist for the 2014 Poets' Prize. Most recently, in 2016, Naomi Replansky, and her life partner, Eva Kollisch were both recipients of a Clara Lemlich Award for Social Activists.

Replansky's work has been included in a wide range of anthologies. Among them are: *Blood to Remember: American Poets in the Holocaust; Inventions of Farewell: A Book of Elegies; Poets of The Non-*

Existent City, Los Angeles in the McCarthy Era; Against Infinity: An Anthology of Contemporary Mathematical Poetry; No More Masks! An Anthology of 20th Century American Woman Poets; and *Between Women: Four Centuries of Love, Romantic Friendship, and Desire.*

Replansky considers herself to be a poet who translates on occasion. She has translated from the French poems by Jules Supervielle; from German, she has translated Bertolt Brecht's poem "Der Sumpf" ("The Swamp") and his play "St. Joan of the Stock Yards"; in addition, she has translated German poems by Matthias Claudius, Hugo von Hofmannsthal, and Nikolaus Lenau, and Yiddish poems by Itzakh Manger.

Replansky's poems are acclaimed for their intensity, precision, and clarity. Writers who have praised her work include George Oppen, B.H. Fairchild, Grace Paley, Marie Ponsot, Philip Levine, Joan Nestle, and Jean Valentine. Replansky has been a factory worker, a lathe operator, an office worker, a computer programmer, and a teacher. Although her poetry is not autobiographical or confessional, her exposure to and interest in the labor movement and anti-racism inform her work, as does her life as a lesbian. Her love for painting watercolors is also manifest in her work. Eva Kollisch, Replansky's partner, is a writer and scholar, and Sarah Lawrence professor emerita.

This interview took place in Replansky's New York, Upper West-Side apartment on November 16, 2013.

Sandra Tarlin: You were born in the Bronx, in 1918. Were your parents connected to the Yiddish community? Did they attend Yiddish theater or read Yiddish newspapers?

Naomi Replansky: No. They both spoke Yiddish fluently, but—unfortunately—they spoke only English at home, so I had to study a bit of Yiddish as an adult. They had this drive to Americanize—they were immigrants. I had an uncle by marriage who loved the Yiddish theater. He was a house painter and used to hang out on 2nd Avenue, and he knew some of those wonderful Yiddish poets like H. Leivick, who I think worked as a wallpaper hanger; my uncle didn't know him as a poet, he knew him as a fellow worker. My parents were secular. We never observed any Jewish holidays: they both came from very Orthodox and quite rigid homes, and this was their rebellion.

ST: I was very touched to read in your 2002 discussion with Edith Chevat in *Bridges* magazine that your mother connected to your poetry, even writing poems down as they came to you ("A Talk with Naomi Replansky," *Bridges*, Vol 9, no.2, Fall 2002).

NR: Yes, if it was nighttime and I was lying in bed and thought of a poem, I'd call her in and she'd write it out. I still have a couple of pages in her handwriting.

ST: Was she interested in literature in general?

NP: No, though she had a scholarly bent. She had worked full-time supporting the family, really, because my father was out of work for a long time. She was an immigrant, she came from a Russian shtetl when she was about twelve, and she had gone to the Eron Preparatory School, which catered to immigrants in those days. Then she got a job as a bookkeeper and then, till her retirement, as a secretary in a school in East Harlem. While working full time and raising her children, she went to Hunter College at night for years and accumulated enough credits to get a B.A when she was about 56.

My father, who never had any schooling at all except for going to Hebrew school in the shtetl when he was a child, read Tolstoy and other books on his own.

ST: How did you find a love for poetry?

NP: [Laughter] there were not many books in the house. I remember a set of books, *The Legends of the Jews* by Louis Ginzberg, they had apocryphal stories, legends, parables. There was also *The Library of Wit and Humor*, which I devoured. It was a 19th century English edition, supposedly funny. There were some poems in there, but it was mainly satirical and political work.

ST: Do you remember the first poem that really moved you?

NP: Yes. Well, I wouldn't say they moved me. Yes, I remember my first poems very well. There was one little book, children's poetry, it was a blue book, one poem in it was "Three jolly Welsh men. . ." I remember another phrase in it, "Snug as a bug in a rug." Nursery rhymes intrigued me very much. I learned many *Mother Goose* rhymes that stuck with me all of my life, they were of course a great influence. My mother somehow picked up a book by Kipling, *Barrack-Room Ballads*. I was about ten when I read that. Kipling, no one likes him because he was an imperialist, but he had this very strong rhythmic sense which I liked. And he was in favor of the soldier, "Tommy Atkins." That was the nickname for the poor boot soldier, the private, the ordinary soldier. Kipling wrote, 'While it's Tommy this, an' Tommy that, an' 'Tommy, fall be'ind,' / But it's 'Please to walk in front, sir' when there's trouble in the wind. . ." ("Tommy"). So this was another poetic influence.

Also when I was 10 or 11, an aunt of mine gave me an anthology by Louis Untermeyer, who was then the big anthologist. She found it in a fire sale, I remember—some of the pages were warped by water. I think this book was *Modern American and British Poetry,*. It was quite wide-ranging and opened up for me a whole new world of poets, techniques, and adventurous themes and possibilities.

But the most important book, with the greatest and most enduring influence in my childhood, was *The Cry for Justice: An Anthology of Social Protest*, edited by Upton Sinclair. It contained short extracts from world literature, ancient to contemporary, about poverty and exploitation, from a Socialist viewpoint.

ST: Have you and your partner ever traveled together to Eastern or Central Europe.

NR: Yes, we went to Austria together—Eva went several times.

ST: I am interested in how you came to write the poem "Korczak and the Orphans" (*Collected Poems* 131).[1]

NR: Well, he was a heroic figure. I read his books and I was very moved by the fact that he could have escaped by leaving his doomed orphans behind. But I consider that poem of mine

---

1 All of Naomi Replansky's poem's quoted in this interview are taken from Replansky, Naomi. *Collected Poems*. Black Sparrow Press, 2012.

too weak in comparison with the subject. It should have been a grander poem. When you choose a large subject like that. . . .

ST: Joan Nestle wrote on her blog about your rediscovering at the Lesbian Herstory Archives two of your first published poems in an anthology *Contemporary American Women Poets* edited by Tooni Gordi.

NR: Yes, it was published in 1936. I wrote the poem earlier, when I was about 15.

ST: That's pretty daring—publishing lesbian poems in 1936.

NR: Strangely, it never entered my mind that it was daring. It ["You with the Roses"][2] was quite explicit, (*Contemporary American Women Poets* 42) too. But I sort of had blinders on—who reads poetry? Not my mother! By the way, I had never owned the anthology. They didn't send me a copy, and I didn't have the money to buy the book. It wasn't until I met Joan and she was showing me around the archives that I saw the book. I told her, "I am in that anthology," and she got very excited.

ST: It seems like you were one of the earliest American lesbian poets. You certainly broke a silence.

NR: I wasn't even aware of that. I just didn't think about it. I didn't think that my mother would even see it [laughter]. I don't think I told my parents, you see. There was this poetry and it went out into the world. It was almost this big abstraction—I didn't even think that people I actually knew would read anything I wrote.

ST: It sounds healthy.

NR: It depends. I wasn't political in that sense. I was quite political about other things. I was quite focused about ending racial injustice. I didn't think of my lesbian identity as particularly distinguishing me. I thought it was a unique private thing. I didn't think of it as a cause.

ST: What happened in the 1970's when Lesbian poets did connect their identity with a new lesbian feminist discourse and

2 Replansky, Naomi. "You with the Roses." *Contemporary American Women Poets: An Anthology of Verse by 113 Living Women.* Edited by Tooni Gordi. Henry Harrison, 1936, p. 42.

tried to obtain rights for the lesbian and gay community. For example, Audre Lorde and Adrienne Rich began to write essays. Did this change your relationship to your poetry and to the lesbian and gay community?

NR: No. When I met Joan Nestle in the late 1960's I became more aware of the existence of lesbian communities. I was very much involved with the Left but somehow, as I said, this was not my cause. But Joan's openness, warmth, and courage were all inspiring. As was the community she had built in her New York apartment.

ST: Many people refer to you as a self-taught poet; I am interested in your practice. Do you have anyone who you consider a mentor?

NR: William Blake. William Blake and Mother Goose [laughter].

ST: Can you talk about Blake a little bit. Is there a favorite poem of Blake's?

NR: His short poems, not the long mystical ones. Those short poems of his, so rich and so simple, so many layers to them. So hard to communicate the magic, "Oh, rose thou art sick…" (Blake "The Sick Rose")

ST: "Fire in the City" (*Collected Poems* 82) and "In the Broken City" (86) both place me in the Bronx and remind me of Blake. I was very moved reading these poems.

NR: Do you live in the Bronx? When I lived in the Bronx it was like we were living in little villages. I realize now how little I knew of the other neighborhoods.

ST: No, I don't live in the Bronx; I teach at Bronx Community College. I had a student who described to me a huge fire where the apartment building she lived in burned down. It all still continues.

NR: Yes.

ST: Did particular incidents prompt you to write these poems.

NR: Actually "Fire in the City"(*Collected Poems* 82) was started when as an adult I went with a friend to look at the house I lived in as a kid in the East Bronx, on 179th Street. We used to live on the third floor. I remember that because my sister had polio, she had a big heavy brace on, and my mother had to carry her up and down the stairs. It [the house] was now cut off at the second floor. There had been a big fire. The first floor was still inhabited. That gave me a very eerie feeling and that went into this poem.

"Broken City," that was Beirut. Beirut at that time was being bombed and destroyed as a city. The Bronx, ravaged by fire and poverty, was also somewhere in my mind in that image.

ST: You worked in a factory. Was it during World War II?

NR: I worked in an office during the first year of the War. I forget exactly when I started in the factory. I was a lathe operator. I continued to operate a lathe after the War.

ST: You have two poems about that period: "Factory Poem" (84) and "The Factory Girl's Farewell" (122).

Photo courtesy of Naomi Replansky

Naomi Replansky circa 1974.

NR: "When I Melt Down" (59) was directly connected to the experience. This big lathe that I operated was also part of the foundry. One time I was assigned to do some lathe work in the foundry, I was asked to work in wood—I had worked in steel mainly. It was the handle of a machine in wood; they take that little wood model and they put it in sand and it makes an impression; then they remove it and pour the molten metal into the sand box and it takes the shape of the model.

ST: It sounds like very careful detailed work.

NR: I wasn't doing the pouring; I saw it being done. All I did was make the wooden model. But seeing that done, and the larger fires and molten metal all around . . . was what gave me the metaphor.

ST: It is very sensual poem.

> When I Melt Down
>
> When I melt down in your furnace
> I want to take shape in your mold.
> Blast me, cast me, change me,
> Before the wind turns to cold.
>
> Look, from the red-hot center
> I lift up my white-hot face.
> My nose finds its bridge as always,
> My eyes flow back into place.
>
> Neither destroyed nor diamond
> I walk from the core of your flame,
> The rain does not hiss when it hits me,
> And I answer to my old name. (59)

ST: In my mind, the speaker moves from fulfilled desire back to control. There is kind of cockiness to the poem and sexual independence. The four line stanzas and the b/d rhyme scheme give the poem a ballad-like feel, celebratory, heroic, and, perhaps, a bit wistful. The craft of the poem, the precisely constructed metaphor, provides a container to hold and shape lesbian love.

Do you consider "When I Melt Down" a celebration of lesbian desire? This poem was written in 1944 and originally published in

Ring Song, 1952. Where you aware of its breaking a silence when the poem was published?

NR: Well, I was writing an erotic poem. I did not consider it only a lesbian poem. I am happy whoever claims a poem as speaking for her or his heart. That is the reader's choice and power.

ST: Will you please speak about the poem "In the Woods" (96)? The poem, starting with the title, seems to read like a frightening fairytale. The unidentified figures are lost and unable to help each other. When one reaches stanza 2 the reader discovers that the woods need not be scary but the figures are only free of fear when they leave each other. Do you consider this a lesbian poem? The poem is from *The Dangerous World,* and starts with "They walked in the world together" (100). How are you playing with the idea of the dangerous world in this poem?

> They walked in the world together
> And came to the end of play.
> Each of them clung to the other
> And each pushed the other away.
>
> That forest was not so scary,
> And two should be warmer than one.
> But each was so scared for the other
> They shivered in spite of the sun.
>
> And each so resembled the other,
> Fear saw only its twin.
> Neither could harbor the other,
> Though skin touched answering skin. (Stanzas 1-3 96)

NR: Yes, this to me is more of a "lesbian" poem—more autobiographical, if you will. Several clues: the conflation of the self with the other—the doubling of fragility in a hostile world—seem to reflect also the physical sameness—. The poem simply tells of (sings of) the ending of an already tortured relationship.

ST: In the poem "The Oasis"(67) there is a mature mind questioning how the gift of a lover and intellectual companion has come to her later in life. The sober mind questions but the newly awakened mind answers. There is a movement within the poem from "I thought I held a fruit cupped in my hand" to "I thought I slipped into a hidden room / out of harsh light," to "I thought I touched a mind that fitted mine / as bodies fit. . .," and finally "I thought the desert ended and I felt / the fountains leap." The body, heart, and mind, come together in this relationship—much to the surprise of the speaker.

The poem "The Oasis" (67) seems to form an arc with "When I Melt Down" (59) and "In the Woods" (96). Were you aware when putting together the *Collected Poems* of the evolving voice of a lesbian speaker, that in your collected works, one thing, among many, is this awareness and reflection of lesbian love at different stages?

NR: Well, a careful reader might come up with that thought of continuous change and evolution. But in the writing, each poem became a world in itself. I wrote at different times, under different circumstances, myself as protagonist in some poems (as in this one); myself as observer or universalist in others.

ST: The union of the body, heart, and mind in "The Oasis" reminds me of the metaphysical poets. Were you influenced by any of the metaphysical poets during the course of your writing life or specifically in relation to these poems?

NR: Yes, I certainly had their music in my head. It comes out almost unbidden. George Herbert is one poet who must have influenced this poem indirectly.

ST: Do you mind discussing with me your poem "The Sightseers"? (27).

NR: "The Sightseers" was inspired when I was living in Paris. I went with a friend to an all-male, enormous dancehall. I went, more or less, as a sightseer. Actually I had an emotional desire to see it. This was in the puritanical 1940's. It was crowded with hundreds of men—many of them in sailors' uniforms. First I felt the excitement of all that openness and intensity; and that excitement became an ironic observation of the crowd of tourists there as sightseers, it became like a dramatic abstraction of two worlds and of society's judgments.

ST: Another poem that I was drawn to was "Oscar Wilde in Reading Gaol" (107-108).

NR: Oh, yes, I should have mentioned Oscar Wilde's "The Ballad of Reading Gaol." I was very much affected by that poem. I think I first read an extract in the Louis Untermeyer anthology. I was a child when I read it and I didn't know why he was in jail. I remembered that poem for many years. As an adult I read a very good biography of Wilde, quite thorough (Richard Ellmann, *Oscar Wilde*, 1987). That inspired me to create this –serious--pastiche. I use the rhythms of the original.

ST: I was also very taken with how you used "the three-plank bed," you took that from the original.

NR: Yes, I got that from the biography.

ST: Your poems make me think of folk music and the blues. Did this influence start in the sixties or earlier?

NR: NR: It started in the thirties. When I was in high school I came across-- I don't know what happened to that book—Francis James Child's *English and Scottish Popular Ballads*, it was a collection of these border ballads and I loved reading them. That was really an influence. Much later there was the folk song craze. The ballad always felt very natural to me, as did so many folk songs. And jazz was in the air, and in my feet—though I couldn't dance well.

An important thing for me was to turn on the radio one day, I was fourteen, and to hear Marian Anderson singing "Sometimes I Feel Like a Motherless Child" — that was one of the greatest artistic epiphanies I ever had. Beautiful. Beautiful. That would be a goal of mine: to write a poem that has that kind of simplicity and emotional power.

ST: Stevie Smith—was she an influence?

NR: No, but she was a fellow spirit. I was already shaped when I read her. One of her poems has become really well-known here.

ST: "Not Waving but Drowning"?

NR: Yes. I wrote her a fan letter in the 50's or 60's, which is what I tend to do if there is something that really gets to me. She answered and we had a correspondence. I went to see her when I was in England. I wouldn't say she was an influence but, as I said, she was a fellow spirit. I admire her work.

Naomi Replansky and Eva Kollisch in 1996.

Photo courtesy of Naomi Replansky

ST: When George Oppen, the Objectivist poet, was alive, he gave you a lot of praise. You were friends with him?

NR: Yes, he wrote to me from Mexico. A man named Charles Humboldt who was a Marxist critic liked my first book, *Ring Song*, very much. It was published in 1952 and he showed it to George Oppen in Mexico and then George wrote me a letter. Then George and Mary moved back to the United States. We got to know each other though we lived at opposite ends of the country.

ST: In the *Nation Magazine*, the critic L.S. Denbo said of Oppen, that he "never believed that politics could be made into poetry or, conversely that poetry could have any effect on social conditions." ("Georg Oppen" poetryfoundation.org). What do you think about that statement?

NR: Well, that's hard to answer. What is meant by "politics"? But, in general, I disagree with Oppen. I think immediately of some wonderful poems about what could be called "politics"— Shelley's "Masque of Anarchy," Brecht's "To Those Born Later," Yeats's "Easter Sunday," Heinrich Heine. . . The list is long.

ST: So, you didn't have any mentor except Blake?

NR: [laughter] I loved other writers but, yes, you might say he was my mentor.

ST: You didn't share your work? You worked in private?

NR: I shared my work with friends, they weren't necessarily poets. There was George Oppen but we didn't discuss individual poems.

ST: The poet Marie Ponsot in her 2009 collection *Easy* dedicates the poem "We Own the Alternative" to you and the Older Women's Network, OWN. Might you talk some about this group of women and the part that it played in your life?

NR: My partner Eva started OWN, Older Women's Network in about 2000. It was made up mostly of artists, writers, social work-ers. . . Now our ranks are thinning because people die. . . We've been meeting for thirteen years and Marie came to some meetings.

ST: The organization is social? Political?

NR: Social. We are more or less in agreement politically—New York liberals.

ST: What is some of the current discussion?

NR: Well we talk about different things, different subjects. It is a little bit like consciousness raising. Our last meeting we got on the topic of anger. Other times, a lot of health issues come up. When we first started people were healthy, but now. . .

ST: You are 98. That is pretty incredible! 98 years!

NR: Well, nothing to boast about.

ST: What are some of the issues you discuss? For example, do you discuss the economy?

NR: Since we see things alike in the group, we don't repeat the news to each other. We help each other out as much as we can.

ST: You have been friends with the poets Jane Cooper and Jean Valentine?

NR: Yes, I met them through Eva, she taught literature at Sarah Lawrence for thirty years. She was a close friend of Grace Paley's. That is actually how Eva and I met, at a reading that Grace gave, and Grace introduced us to each other after the reading.

ST: You were influenced by the haiku?

NR: I love the haiku and the tanka, but I read them only in translation. . ., I don't know that I was consciously influenced, and I don't count out the syllables. I have written some short poems but of course they are not really haiku.

ST: Are you writing now.

NR: No. No, I always have periods where . . . . It may come back, I don't know.

ST: Is there a collection of translations by you waiting to be published?

NP: No. I've done translations only every now and then, out of admiration for the original or for fun or because it was a challenge. It was haphazard.

ST: Are you reading anything now?

NR: Oh, I always read, but I am not reading a lot of poetry. No.

ST: What are you reading?

NR: I mean I read the old poetry, the poetry I already love. And once in a while I read a new, profound, musical voice in a poem, and get all excited. At the moment I am reading a book, not poetry, by Andrew Solomon, *Far from the Tree.* It's a study of parents and unusual children who have cognitive, physical, or psychological differences. The children don't fit the so-called normal categories and each chapter deals with the family of an exceptional child; one chapter is on dwarfism, one on prodigies, one on schizophrenia, one on transgender, etc. He describes the complex relationships of the children, parents, and siblings, and the attitudes and often false assumptions of society. Solomon himself is gay and went through a period of terrible depression. It's a fascinating book.

ST: It sounds wonderful.

NR: He describes the way parents feel, both the history [of the difference] and the relationship of the parents with their children. So I am reading that and I am reading slowly, very slowly, a book in German by Ruth Kluger, who was a child in Austria, a Jewish child in Austria who was imprisoned in Auschwitz with her mother, and later in several labor camps. Survived. Came here when she was seventeen and is a brilliant poet. Her first poem was conceived in Auschwitz when she was 13, and it is a wonderful poem called "The Chimney" about the crematorium at Auschwitz. She didn't write it down because of course they had no papers or pencils but it was published just right after the war. In 1944, a friend of mine, who was a German political refugee, showed it to me and asked me to translate it. I had only high school German, but I managed, I did a translation of it.

Sixty years later, and I assumed this child had died in Auschwitz, Eva and I were visiting Vienna and there was an exhibit in the Town Hall about Austria's anti-Semitic history (an enormous history!). In a small ante-room they had a little pile of books, and I see this book, and I see the name, I remembered that name, for sixty years I had remembered that name, and I thought, "Oh, it must be a common name." But I trembled. I opened the book and there was the poem I had translated, the German poem. So, that's the background.

Ruth Kluger (known in Germany as Ruth Klueger) has published a lot of books. One of the latest is a book which contains her poems with her own commentary. A poet may do it on other poets, but is rare for a poet to comment on herself. I'm reading it slowly because my German is not that fluent. Those are the two books I am reading right now

My partner Eva Kollisch was rescued from the Nazis in Austria by a *Kindertransport* when she was fourteen. She wrote two books about her experience. She came to Staten Island at 15, where she became friendly with a group of Trotskyists, and joined the movement. She wrote a book called *Girl in Movement*—it's about her teen-age experience in the Trotskyist movement. Her second book is a collection of essays and personal stories about her experiences in Austria after Hitler took over. This book was translated into German, and she won a major literary prize in Austria (the Theodor Kramer Preis, in 2012). When she went to Austria to get the prize, Ruth Kluger heard her being interviewed on the radio and came to Eva's reading and liked the book very much and they became friendly. So, it's a great circle.

ST: I am glad I asked!

NR: [Laughter]

ST: So, you just did a reading with Edward Field. That sounds like an interesting friendship, too.

NR: I like him very much. He is a fine poet. He has written beautifully about his relationship with his partner Neil.

ST: I think that the fact that you are a lesbian is implicit in a lot of your collected works.

NR: Yes.

ST: I think that George Oppen was correct in saying that you are one of America's "most brilliant poets (Back Cover, *Collected Works*)." Thank you, Naomi, for the interview.

OBITUARIES

IRENE R. WEISS, AUGUST 30, 1926 – OCTOBER 14, 2016

Irene Weiss died at the age of ninety on October 14th under Hospice care at the home she shared with her partner and spouse, Michelle de Beixedon in Sequim, Washington. In spite of a long struggle against failing health, which she endured bravely, Irene was able to joyously celebrate her wedding anniversary in July and her ninetieth birthday in August with numerous friends and family from near and far.

Irene was born, the much-cherished daughter of Russian Jewish immigrant parents, on August 30, 1926 in Pittsburgh Pennsylvania. An avid reader from an early age, Irene skipped several grades in school and spent every available free moment in the great library in her city built by Andrew Carnegie. She remembers as a young child sitting at the kitchen table in the home they shared with an extended family of aunts, uncles and cousins, teaching her shy and lovely mother to speak, read and write the English language. Voracious reading and a profound love of literature would be a hallmark of her life from then on.

It was in high school that Irene began to get intimations of her authentic sexuality and through a series of intense crushes on girls, experimentation and her omnivorous reading she realized that she was what was then termed a homosexual. In the 1940's, decades before the gay liberation movements of the late 60's and early 70's, when Irene entered nurses training under the government sponsored Cadet Nursing Program, she began to openly claim her identity as a lesbian.

Irene told her parents for whom, of course, this was extremely difficult, and they tried to dissuade her from a life that they were sure would bring their beloved daughter nothing but heartbreak and ruin. Realizing that she could no longer stay at home and with nursing degree in hand, Irene moved to New York City to work in a hospital by day and to explore the Village and it's gay life by night, where for the first time she met other out lesbians.

In 1951 New York City winters prompted Irene and a friend to drive west in her first car to the warmer climes of Southern California. In Los Angeles, she found the career that she would be passionate about for the rest of her working life. She began work first as a nurse, then as a supervisor, then as a director, then as an advocate at the state level, establishing one of the first nursing home accreditation associations the industry, and finally as a partner in a nursing home business.

After a series of relationships, which, as Irene said, "are often how we find out who we are as lesbians, and find ourselves as lesbians" in what was then an outlaw world, Irene met Marilyn Murphy, the woman who would become her long time partner. Together they would become theorists and leading activists in the fledgling second wave of the women's and the lesbian feminist movements in Southern California and nationally. With Irene supporting Marilyn's work and writing throughout, they would be instrumental in founding the Califia Collective, an educational and consciousness raising "boot camp" for women leading workshops on issues of sexisms, homophobia, racism, anti-Semitism, and classism that, over the course of its existence, impacted the lives of many hundreds of women.

Inspired to take their program on the road, as related in Marilyn's book *"Are You Girls Traveling Alone?"* they would ultimately work in several women's communities: first at the Pagoda in St. Augustine, Florida, then at Superstition Mountain Resort in Arizona and finally at Discover Bay in Washington State. Throughout her life, Irene's generosity would support numerous organizations and individuals whose goal was to improve the lives of women and lesbians. Tragically, in the late nineties, Marilyn's health began to deteriorate and, over five years, she lost the ability to do her work. Irene took loving care of her during this long and very difficult period for both of them until Marilyn's death in 2004.

Life was not over, however, for Irene. Although her health, too, had become greatly compromised and she needed the help of many devoted friends, in 2011 at the age of 85, to their mutual surprise and astonishment, Irene met Michelle de Beixedon, a retired college professor and the woman who would become her lover, companion, partner and spouse, caring for her until her death in October of this year. During their too short time together they found a deep love and happiness that neither of them had expected.

In her final birthday toast to Irene, Michelle said, "I love you for your wisdom. I have never met anyone who has a keener intelligence nor a more genuine and profound passion for the life of the mind than you do. I love you for your dignity, for your honesty, your integrity, and your courage, for your steadfast insistence upon openly living the truth of who you are regardless of the costs. I love your radical lesbian feminist vision, a vision born of a serious and a lifelong commitment to live beyond the dehumanizations of sexism, of homophobia, of racism, of classism and the ubiquitous violence that diminishes women everywhere. I love you for the ageless and infectious curiosity and delight in life itself. Most of all I love you for your great and tender heart and it certainly doesn't hurt that I am, as you know, ravished by the package it's wrapped in . . . ."

Each of us can only hope to live a life as long and as rich and as full as Irene's. She will be lovingly remembered and celebrated by numerous friends, family and colleagues whose lives she touched deeply in so many ways. —Michelle de Breixedon, Ph.D.

SUSAN LEVINKIND, APRIL 24, 1942 – OCTOBER 29, 2016

Susan Levinkind, 74, a generous and loving spouse, mother, grandmother, activist and friend to many, died on October 29, 2016, of a seizure disorder accompanying Lewy Body dementia, at home in Oakland, California.

Susan came out in her late 30s, inspired by lesbian activism in Northampton, Massachusetts. She had always been an active participant in the movements for racial and economic justice, as well as the anti-nuclear and peace movements. She engaged with delight in lesbian life, supporting cultural, legal and political causes for the last 40 years of her life. She was a stalwart supporter of *Sinister Wisdom* since moving to the Bay Area in 1989.

Born in Holyoke, Massachusetts, she got her library degree from Columbia, and J.D. from Western New England College of Law. She worked first as a librarian in New York and Amherst, MA, then as «the lesbian lawyer» of Northampton. Many of her clients still remember her dedication to their cases and the steady calm with which she helped them. When Northampton officials wouldn›t issue a permit for an LGBT march in the 1980s, she contacted the ACLU and worked to make sure every business in the city signed a petition to city hall supporting the march – which has taken place annually every since.

She moved to California in 1989 where she participated in numerous lesbian groups (and spent several years hosting a Jewish lesbian atheist vegetarian seder), worked as a legal librarian for

California Rural Legal Assistance and the Superior Court of San Jose, as well as being "the lesbian tax mom" for over 100 clients after her "retirement." She also co-wrote the book on Legal Research for Nolo Press that was adopted by law schools all over the U.S.

Traveling always pleased her—especially going to the ocean. Susan helped keep the local library and lesbian-owned bookstore in business with her love of reading. And she responded with joy and energy at any women's cultural event—many friends reported their pleasure at seeing her dance with Elana at the Charlotte Maxwell Complementary Care Clinic's benefit concert this last September.

While dementia is grievous disease, Susan's core of kindness and love persisted until the end. In March of 2016, she went to an International Women's Day concert given by the Rockin' Solidarity Labor Chorus and, stirred by hearing the labor and social justice songs of her youth, immediately signed up, becoming a valued member during her last six months. She was able to perform with them twice.

A life-long activist, she took her daughter, Andrea, to Vietnam War and anti-nuke protests. For over 25 years she was the tireless office worker for the journal *Sinister Wisdom*, making sure the subscriber lists were up to date, the proofreading got done, the books balanced—one of the most cheerful and dedicated behind-the-scenes volunteers ever. She co-organized senior and disabled services for the San Francisco Dyke March for eight years, where lesbians who needed any kind of assistance could recognize Susan as the woman wearing the cat-in-the-hat hat. After turning 60, she tirelessly promoted Bay Area and National Old Lesbians Organizing for Change, serving on both the local and, briefly, on the national board.

Susan was the woman who, at any social or political event, would sit beside women who seemed ill at ease and made them comfortable. She was consistently generous and would do anything for her clients, family and friends. She was given the legendary Pat Bond Old Dykes Award for her many contributions to lesbian community in 2007.

She is survived by her loving spouse, Elana Dykewomon, her closest friend, Casey Fisher, her daughter, Andrea Cook, her son-in-law Scott Cook, and grandsons Sam and Adam. —Elana Dykewomon

RUTH MOUNTAINGROVE, FEBRUARY 21, 1923 – DECEMBER 18, 2106

On the left—Ruth as subject at Ovular V.
On the right—Ruth Teaching the 4x5 at Ovular VI.

Ruth Mountaingrove, lesbian-feminist poet, photographer, composer, publisher, musician, playwright, painter, and women's land pioneer, died peacefully on December 18, 2016, at Ida Emmerson Hospice House in Eureka, California.

Ruth was born Ruth Shook on February 21, 1923 in Philadelphia Pennsylvania, daughter of Edith Shelling and Herbert Shook. She graduated from Kutztown State Teachers College in 1945, and in 1946 published her first book of poetry, *Rhythms of Spring*, and married Bern Ikeler. They had five children. After her 1965 divorce, she became involved in feminism, and met her future partner, Jean Mountaingrove. In 1971, she and two of her children joined Jean at Mountain Grove, an intentional community in rural southern Oregon.

Ruth and Jean became central figures in the Southern Oregon women's land movement, publishing *WomanSpirit Magazine* and *The Blatant Image* and organizing women's photography "Ovulars." She published her second book of poetry, *For Those who Cannot Speak*, and *The Turned-on Woman Songbook*.

In 1986 Ruth moved to Arcata, California. She continued her photography and poetry as well as participating in many community activities: *Through the Eyes of Women* and the Women's Radio Collective on KHSU, the Ink People, *Senior News*, volunteering at the library, and serving on the Grand Jury. She earned two masters degrees at Humboldt State, in Art and Photography and in Theater Production and Dramatic Writing. She sang at many local events and wrote for the *L-Word*, a local lesbian publication, for many years. She also wrote for national and international publications, including *off our backs*, *Sinister Wisdom*, and *Rain and Thunder*, and published a third poetry book *I Remind Myself*.

Ruth is survived by her children, Kim (Donna), Jeffrey, and Heather Ikeler, grandchildren Jeffrey (Tanya) and Hannah Ikeler, and great-granddaughter Evelyn Grace Ikeler.

As Ruth aged, a circle of committed friends and caregivers helped her stay in her home and then supported her through her transition. Ruth especially counted on Sue Hilton, whom she affectionately called her "manager." The PACE program provided invaluable support, and dealt cheerfully with the complexities of working with our group.

Ruth was creative, funny, inspirational, courageous, caring, independent, outspoken, and determined. She is missed in her many different communities.

Her photographs are archived in the Ruth Mountaingrove collection at the University of Oregon Libraries Special Collections. Ruth's friends encourage donations in her name to any organization supporting women or the arts. If you have stories to share or want more info, you can contact Sue at suejh@humboldt1.com.

Maggie Jochild, August 5, 1955 – January 6, 2107

Maggie Jochild (Meg Barnett), poet, activist, blogger, novelist, and luminous radical lesbian feminist voice died on January 6, 2017. Maggie lent her talents to us as a beacon for lesbian life and community. A wordsmith, unafraid to tackle the hard issues, she began developing her word skills in rural Texas under the push of a grade school teacher and her own fierce determination to excel in English. Maggie was a chronicler of lesbian community, relationships, and self, she developed a clear voice forwarding the progression of lesbian culture, from working against police violence in the streets of San Francisco, to writing and conversing with other lesbians on a blog called Meta Watershed and many places in between.

Maggie's vision can be seen in the story, "Trapeze," published in *Sinister Wisdom* 16 (Summer 1981). The narrative elicits vivid pictures recounting dream lessons, teaching how to swing on a trapeze. These dream lessons are metaphors for navigating the waters of a lesbian relationship, as well as living in women's community. The prose is resplendent and exact, clear and mesmerizing. Maggie wrote: "As I fly out again, I am aware of the air brushing into the scoop of my body. In the split second at the end of my flight, I relax my legs and let my body go convex, readjusting the muscles. It is enough. I am returning, blindly, my back to the platform." The lesson illuminates the fear of falling without a net; the strength of women's community, the woven cord of safety

In "Why There Are No Skeletons of Wimmin Martyrs," published in *Sinister Wisdom* 11 (Fall 1979), Maggie wrote about living in a lesbian collective in Durango, Colorado. The prose is a poetic vision of lesbian lives: "And when we love, she is a girl again, a wild-hearted girl who loved too greatly for her time but not for mine. I am trying, very hard, to make up for the decades she lived with a broken heart. I think I can do this because I loved her for decades, reading the lines both written and silent that told how like me she was."

At *Poets & Writers*, Maggie describes herself as writing "narrative poetry about the effects of having lived in 36 different places so far, of being raised in a post-war godhelpus traditional nuke fam enduring haphazard poverty, of coming out to herself as a lesbian and a poet at age nine during the summer of 1965, of joining the Revolution during the 70's, and deciding to never again suffer fools gladly during the Reagan administration." She continued describing her work as being "about loving women without restraint, about choosing to be an unreconstructed feminist, about traveling the roads of race and class traitorhood, about being the first generation to name and stand up against child abuse, about mothering, godmothering and grandmothering, about a failing body and a ferocious spirit. She writes with the unshackled, unhurried speech of her people, Southern dirtfarmer bookish renegades since 1609. She writes with faith and humor the kinds of truth that you have wanted to hear but weren't sure you could bear."

Maggie's work appears in numerous anthologies and feminist journals including *Albatross, America Review, Ashphodel, Aunt Lute, Borderlands, Bridges, Common Lives, Earth's Daughters, Lalitamba, Malachite & Agate, Natural Bridge, PMS: poemmemoirstory, Poetry Motel, Poetry Now, Rockhurst Review*, and *Sinister Wisdom*. She received two Loving Lesbians Poetry Award from the Astraea Lesbian Writers Fund.

Maggie died at home in Austin, Texas among community and her beloved. And though Maggie's voice lives on, her heartfelt physical presence, remembered by many, is sorely missed. – Roberta Arnold

BOOK REVIEWS

"A Generous Intelligence Displayed in all Its Sensual Grace"[1]

Collected Poems
Naomi Replansky
Black Sparrow/Godine, 2012
Paperback, $17.95 - 128 pages

Reviewed by Joan Nestle

From "A Visit to a Zoo:"

> See the poet,
> Will it bite?
> Sometimes if aroused.
>
> Feeds? on anything.
> A word ate a tear,
> Ate a laugh, ate love,
> Swallowed anger, gulped down hope.
> A word ate a word
> Made of venom, of honey
> And still came back hungry... (1937) (40)

To write of the poetry of Naomi Replansky with the looming figure of Trump and his minions mounting to their heights

---

1 From Replansky's poem, "The Human Intellect Divine," (written about 1990s, and written not about herself) p.142.

of power is to remember once again that in the cadences of our poets lives our hope. Replansky's poetry is born of historical displacements that create a seeing heart, a singing heart, a raging heart full of the complexities of our cruelties to each other, our longing for each other, inevitabilities taken on sometimes with wit, sometimes with bite. Find her *Collected Poems* treasure the rare interviews she has given like the one is this issue, and find her voice, on line, her face looking right at you as she speaks the lines of her life. This brief essay is to call your attention to her work, now, when we need her so much. For so many years, Replansky has been crafting a way to speak of large social hurts with not one wasted word, with a profound control of language. In 1950 she wrote,

Foreigner
He is alone and unarmed
And has no vessel for his vanity.
His curse is spoken, but nothing trembles.
His praise like rain runs down the gutters.

Laughter seizes him and he is silent.
God shakes him, he hides it in a stare.
And he can change nothing where he passes
Though he walk barefoot through bristling events.

A room, a street, a war
Gather within and sinew him for speech
Richer than this, but who will hear him out.
O who will hear him unto nakedness.
(1950) (48)

Notice how the poet so deeply feels her own privilege of having language when those deemed unseeable, lose all impact on the air around them. Trump is vanity incarnate; the poet is humbled by the cost of historical calamities. In this time of rampant chauvenisms, find the poets.

Now I will confess I cannot write of Naomi Replansky as The Poet. Others will do that much better than me. I must write of Naomi, my friend, whose voice lives with me. The poetry of Naomi Replansky, the person of Naomi Replansky, the wonder of her voice carrying her own poems and then those she loved. We walk in Central Park, close to our then shared neighbourhood on the Upper West Side of New York, when it was still possible to afford to live there and she recites for me Edna St Vincent Millay's "Prayer to Persephone," "Be to her Persephone/all the things I might not be. /Take her head upon your knee/ she that was so proud and wild,/Flippant, arrogant and free,/Is a little lonely child /lost in Hell, Persephone./Take her head upon your knee/Say to her, My dear, my dear/It is not so dreadful here."

Through the decades we walked and always I asked to hear this lament for a lost young love and so much more in that ringing caring voice of my poet friend. I cannot write of Naomi's poetry without speaking of her person, of the living gifts she offers of words that sing for her, or move her, her offerings of them as comfort or laughter or a hint of how to get through. The words move through her, live in her, removed from paper or book, made into her flesh, and then brought into the air to live again. She is as generous with another's poem as she is with her own. Poetry, yes a complex craft, but also a mother's hand upon a fevered brow.

Now with her collected works, now in her 99th year, we can hear all the textures, all the songs, all the internal conversations demanded by an engaged life. We live with the poet as a worker, as political observer, as a young woman with a thin skin, as an old woman who finds a great love that melts the barren places but true to her Bronx Depression born days, she warns herself of the fragility of these new green lands. There is the weight of history in these poems, of exclusions unto death, of people turned to unseen wraiths by those with power, the poet using a language and a rhyme that depict with acute emotional insight the yearning human body encased in uncaring streets, factories, historical places of desolation.

Epitaph: 1945

My spoon was lifted when the bomb came down/That left no face, no hand, no spoon to hold./A hundred thousand died in my home town./This came to pass before my soup was cold.

Through the decades, we have spoken of what is a lesbian poem, a lesbian painting. Now at seventy-seven reading my friend's life work, I see that life makes our poems lesbian. Economic realities make our poems lesbian, the work our hands do or that we see others doing, the realizations of myriad displacements, the joy coming back to life because of another, the lostness of loss, the sorrow for poems not written, the sting of rejections, the debate between a body and time. All the matter of lesbian poetry. Naomi never gives easy answers—there are none for the themes of her poetry, there are none for our lives.

The Six Million

They entered the fiery furnace
And never one came forth.
How can that be my brothers?
But it is true, my sisters.
They entered the fiery furnace
And never one came forth.

No god came down, my brothers,
To breath on them, my sisters.
Their bodies made a mountain
That never touched the Heavens.
Whose lightning struck the killers?
Whose rain drowned out the fires?

My brothers and my sisters,
No angel leaned upon them.
No miracle could shield them
From the cold human hands.

(1946) (20)

Never a fancy woman, never an arrogant poet, never far from her father's worry about how will the rent be paid, Naomi wrote her poems slowly, crafting the music of her worries, her celebrations, her witnessed belittlements, her longing for a more caring world over days, months, years. I remember visiting Naomi in the 1980s in her two-room apartment in the 70s, and here in the second room, was a low wooden desk. In the center of it was the poem of the day or year, so still and so waiting. It was in this same apartment that a few of us studied poetry with Replansky, a rare and moving experience. Never had I been so close to a person who had made poetry her inner life, who brought into the room the remembered words of others as if she was simply breathing. See, I too was a child of the working class Jewish Bronx who slowly through accidents of kindness discovered the poets, the writers, that which was called "literature." Sometime Naomi and I would share cups of a European green tea in that small living room bounded by a window at one end and a hot plate and tiny sink on the other, her kitchen. The richness was all in the shared words, the fineness of the poet's spirit, her generosity in having patience with my roughness.

The rhythms of Replansky's poetry, so often commented on as making her work out of step with the poetic mainstream, now come into their full brilliance. Her words will stay with you, like old friends but demanding to be looked at again and then the wonder of the complexity of her vision of the human heart will break all patterns.

At the end of conversations whether on the phone or in an e-mail, Naomi often writes, "forza" and so I write to all of you—go on with the strength of the caring heart.

Indomitable: The Life of Barbara Grier
Joanne Passet
Bella Books, 2016
Cloth, $28.95 - 338 pages

Reviewed by Jaime Harker

Joanne Passet's *Indomitable: The Life of Barbara Grier* is an essential contribution to lesbian letters and American literary history. Taking advantage of interviews with Grier's partner, Donna McBride, and using McBride's private archival holdings, and well as extensive archival research, Passet provides a detailed portrait of Grier's life and achievements in inventing lesbian literature as a recognizable and lucrative literary category. As the feminist print culture that made Barbara Grier's success possible grows increasingly remote, the biography's thorough treatment of Grier's life and legacy makes a case for her continued importance in queer cultural memory.

Indomitable catalogues Grier's early life in much more detail than she ever revealed in interviews. Her early life of grinding poverty and frequent moves led to an imagined home of sorts in one of the first manifestations of the gay press. Growing up in a Cold War culture with few public references to gay life, Grier became a bibliophile; when she discovered *The Ladder*, the official publication of the Daughters of Bilitis, she found what she considered to be her life's work. Starting with reviews, short stories, and features under many pseudonyms, Grier's most famous *nom de plume* was Gene Damon, who published reviews of books that would be collected in the annual bibliography *The Lesbian in Literature*. Grier wrote for *The Ladder* from 1957 to 1972, working her way up from contributor to book editor to general editor. Along the way, she met many lesbian writers (like Marion Zimmer Bradley and Jane Rule) and readers, ruffled feathers, made enemies, and stole the magazine from the Daughters of Bilitis, along with its super secret mailing list, which would become the foundation for success of Naiad Press.

Her rejection of the "homophile" movement for the lesbian feminist movement lost her the support of a DOB 'angel' who supported *The Ladder*, contributing to its demise. But her connection to the feminist movement, and the young radicals causing trouble (like Rita Mae Brown), led to her most famous public achievement—the creation of Naiad Press. The press began with the financial support of two retired lesbians who had read *The Ladder*, and remained silent partners for many years; one wanted to publish novels and thought Grier could help with distribution. Grier turned this modest publishing venture into a wildly successful publishing enterprise, one that would make lesbian genre fiction the backbone of its success, as well as that of feminist bookstores nationwide. The story of Grier's creation of a solvent company, the many lesbians authors she mentored (and bullied), the network of bookstores she cajoled into carrying Naiad's latest books, and the mailing service she mastered, is sometimes maddening but always entertaining, and it suggests the larger triumph of the Women in Print movement, which created an alternative ecology of lesbian literature before ebooks and Amazon.com made distribution and authorship easier but make getting noticed that much harder.

Passet tells this story with clarity, including here-to-fore unknown details, archival work, and secondary contextualization. The amount of research compressed into unobtrusive footnotes is immense. Sometimes, Passet passes over conflicts and issues with more brevity than I would like—but given how much is here, and how much ground she had to cover, that feels like a trifling objection. Passet has produced a rich and suggestive portrait of Grier, one that will open up legions of new research and will introduce Grier to a new generation of readers, who know lesbian literature only from "lesfic" and online guides. Passet's publication of this book by Bella Books, which bought out Naiad's backlist on Grier's retirement, is fitting, and I can only hope that Bella's distribution acumen will get *Indomitable* the audience it deserves.

We Hunger to Be Hybrid

Catechism: A Love Story
Julie Marie Wade
Noctuary Press, 2016
Paperback, $14.00 - 158 pages

Reviewed by Barrie Jean Borich

Queer women survive such complicated geometries. The base of our triangle is the mess of lived experience, our altitude the still pervasive image of the nice and likeable woman, our vertex the inadequate language we have to describe how we keep making ourselves over.

Julie Marie Wade takes on these formulas and calculations in her book, *Catechism: A Love Story*. A poet and creative nonfiction writer, Wade is one of our best contemporary lyric essayists of lesbian existence, both because her ear is so finally attuned to the nuance of lesbian coming to knowledge and because her voice is so welcoming to the embodied love of the world. In this, her latest work, she makes new a familiar story of breaking away from the expectations put upon the daughter of a conservative Catholic American family after she falls in love with a woman. But while the story may be common, the form of this work—what the author calls a "lyric enterprise"— is refreshingly beautiful. The complicated mathematics of desire and disobedience are, to Wade, not a direct or linear tale, but an experience of transubstantiation that can only be captured through literary hybridity.

In the realm of creative nonfiction literature, hybridity is the act of bringing disparate forms together in the body of new work unbound to genre categories. The formal experimentation is not unlike ways the disobedient female body defies conventional category. Wade writes of merging the devotion and ritual of her sacrament-bound childhood with the ecstatic shattering that comes of reading Adrienne Rich and coming to realize the carefully fitted wedding dress, purchased for the church wedding to her male fiancé, would never make it out of its wrapping. "The hours I had spent with the seamstress," Wade writes. "The moment on the pedestal before a triangle of mirrors. All this for something, for nothing? Who could say? It was easier to postulate the fate of the gown: would it melt in the sun, surrender to moths, be stolen by some Rapunzel-type on the run?" (liii)

Catechism is a slender book that resounds like poetry but reads as a looping and repeating story, accomplishing at once both narrative and song. The book is arranged as a collection of sacraments—Eucharist, Matrimony, Confirmation, and so on— each chapter another rite, rewritten across a body that spans what Wade calls the Before, the After, the Once and the Always. Wade writes of an obedient childhood, her teachers sending notes home reporting not bad behavior but concerns that this child was disturbingly good, overly helpful and too eager to please. She describes her relationship to her fiancé as polite, compliant, and dispassionate, and she revolts only through silent omissions—such as faking her side of their long distance phone sex by watching television or flipping through magazines. She writes of how she was pleased to be passively pleasing him, understanding this time of her life as a given geometry. "My life with a man had been easy to graph, I the abscissa, he the ordinate. Our intersection marked the right angle of tradition—what our parents had done and their parents before them. At a certain moment in time I had been chosen: the perpendicular penetration of my line at a specified point." (xxxii)

Within this geometry—which contains mathematical metaphors, explications and quotations of Adrienne Rich's poetry, fragments of fairy tales, texts of both science and sacrament, and Wades's own ear for startling language—she comes to a profound and life altering splitting. She skips her own wedding in order to take off on a cross-country road trip with the woman—later her wife—she was still only able to describe to family as her friend. "The splitting is easier than the sewing back up, but perhaps intactness is not what the body desires ....I suspect we hunger to be hybrid." (xlii)

Catechism, like any ritual, contains repeating actions that combine to create a sacramental gesture, but through these sacred movements Wade is recalculated by the discovery of her own lesbian body. "Trigonometry is the study of triangles," she writes, "the mapping of deltas, the framing of change." (cxxxi)

This is a book to read and reread for the liturgy it brings to lesbian lives, celebrating the love story itself but also the complex and ongoing reckoning of how we've remade ourselves against the women we were supposed to be.

CONTRIBUTORS

Barbara Esrig moved to Gainesville, FL, in October 1979. That same month she came out and started working as a nurse at the Gainesville Women's Health Clinic and has been politically active in her community since then. In 1999 she became the writer-in-residence in the Shands Arts-in-Medicine program doing oral histories in the hospital and has made listening to people's stories her permanent career.

Barbara Ester is a singer, songwriter, and massage therapist who currently lives in Spartanburg, SC, with her wife, Beth York. She co-created Music for Lesbians in 1987 with her former partner, Bairbe. Their last recording, *HeartSongs*, with Beth York, was produced by Music for Lesbians in 2008.

Barrie Jean Borich is the author of *Body Geographic*, winner of a Lambda Literary Award and *My Lesbian Husband*, recipient of a Stonewall Book Award. She's an associate professor at DePaul University in Chicago where she edits *Slag Glass City*, a digital journal of the urban essay arts.

Beth Marschak grew up in Richmond and was actively engaged in the social change movements of the 1960s and 1970s—Civil Rights, the Women's Liberation Movement, the Ecology Movement, the Peace Movement, and Lesbian and Gay Liberation. She came out as a lesbian in the early 1970s and openly identified as a lesbian in her civil rights and human rights activism. She has served on a number of boards and received many awards for her advocacy work.

Beth York, PhD, MT-BC, is a board-certified music therapist and Professor of Music Therapy at Converse College, a women's college in Spartanburg, SC. Her feminist-informed practice has included work with women survivors of domestic violence, documented in the performance piece "Finding Voice" (*Feminist Perspectives in Music Therapy*, ed. Sue Hadley, Gilsum, NH: Barcelona, 2006). Ladyslipper Music produced her recording *Transformations*, and she performed the instrumental work nationally at Southern, Michigan, New England, and National Women's Music Festivals.

Blanche Jackson quit civil service to take yoga teachers training. Used the retirement fund for a loft in an old building to learn how to split logs, operate a wood stove, and grow food on the roof. Regrets? Nope, just gazing up at the underbelly of the poverty line thinking, "Hmmmmmm, what next?"

Carol J. Kraemer is a community activist and cultural worker who has worked for civil rights in Louisville, KY, for over twenty-five years. In 1988, she co-founded the lesbian rock band Yer Girlfriend. She has worked for the Fairness Campaign and has been active in struggles for workers' rights, immigrant rights, and against police abuse. She currently serves on the board of the Carl Braden Memorial Center, is a co-founder and leadership team member of Louisville Showing Up for Racial Justice, and is the director of the David–Putter Scholarship Fund which provides grants for student activists.

Calla Felicity. Calla Felicity: 1989. Carol Kramer drove us to an open mic in Lexington, where she performed an original Lesbian song for the first time to a roomful of strangers. It's been my life's privilege to audience the art of such gifted, activist Lesbian writers and musicians. A beautiful joy.

Charlene Ball has published short stories, poetry, and academic articles. She is a Hambidge Fellow and held a residency at the Helene Wurlitzer Foundation of New Mexico. Since she retired from Georgia State University in 2009, she spends her time writing and selling antiquarian and collectible books with her wife Libby Ware, an author and bookseller. Charlene's first novel, *Dark Lady: A Novel About Emilia Bassano Lanyer*, will be published in June 2017.

Flash Silvermoon is a nationally known Spiritual Renaissance Woman. She is the author and creator of *The Wise Woman's Tarot* book and deck and a Priestess of the Rainbow Goddess Tradition. She has a monthly radio show *Womanspirit Rising* as well as the weekly *What the Animals Tell Me*. Flash has been stirring the Cauldron in the Lesbian and Feminist Movement since the early 1970s in New York City as well as Florida now. Anyone who has gone to many of the major women's music festivals has seen her tearing it up as a solo artist, as a member of her band Medusa Muzic and the Blues Sisters, and jamming with many other performers. Flash is just as comfortable reading Tarot, doing an Astrological chart, delivering a Past Life Regression, Stone Healing, Flower Essence or Gem Elixer treatment, and of course COMMUNICATING AND TREATING THE BELOVED ANIMALS.

Gail Reeder was a Brasso brat (an army brat) who grew up everywhere. She returned to the South following familial feet to rural North Carolina. She was a grassroots organizer for racial equality and writer of antiwar and feminist articles for the *Quicksilver Times*, *Southern Voice*, *Pulse Magazine*, and other alternative publications. "These days I am more dangerous with a pickax than a gun, but I still keep an eye on the revolution."

Landing in Richmond, VA, following college and graduate schools, **Ginger Starling** joined Other Voices: The Richmond Lesbian and Gay Chorus in 1991 and served as Artistic Director from 1996 to 1999. She moved to Northern Virginia in 1999, played in several area bands, and worked for the Songwriters' Association of Washington, DC. Ginger now lives in Alabama, where she writes music, runs Dapper Otter Productions, and writes for the local LGBTQ community.

Harvest Boward was born and grew up in western Maryland. She came out in the 1970s and lived on women's lands. She lived at Peacemaker Land Trust, Tribeland, OWL Farm, Cabbage Lane, and ARF. Land-based culture is important to her. She is thankful for the influence of her grandmother Miriam of the mountains, Linda Shear's music, and the MAIZE community.

A music lover since her Delaware childhood, **Joyce Hopkins** has always championed women's place in the music world. Ever since her first band (in Europe in the 1960s) decided it could not make use of her skill on trumpet, Joyce has played electric bass in multiple ensembles. When she arrived in Louisville in the 1970s, she quickly found her place among other women musicians and activists, and River City Wimmin stepped forward to inspire, empower, and entertain. RCW evolved into Tiffany, a band name chosen to suggest the special light created by viewing diverse music through the unique lens of a fully professional full-time women's band. After several years of full-time band touring, Joyce and other Tiffany members went on to play in a variety of configurations over the coming decades. Joyce continues to live in Louisville, continues to support women in music, continues to play bass with friends, and is even toying with returning to the trumpet.

Jenna Weston is an artist, writer, and teacher. She grew up in Michigan and came out there in the late 1970s. Since then Jenna has been committed to the creation of Lesbian community and culture, contributing her art and writing to numerous women's and Lesbian publications. She now lives in North Florida.

Kathleen "Corky" Culver. Music and dance and poetry coursing through the nervous system nourishes happiness, spirituality, healing, something to live for, something to share, from the back porch gathering, to the stage. Let there be art. Political movements full of art have survived struggle to love and laugh.

LauRose Dancingfire Felicity is a cis-gendered femme lesbian teacher and attorney who has worked on behalf of lesbian mothers, abused women, and children. She and her wife, Calla, have two beautiful adopted African American daughters. She would personally dismantle state-supported school segregation if she could. She loved working on the Yer Girlfriend piece for this edition of *Sinister Wisdom* and is currently completing a new version of the *Tarot, The Bible of the Witches Resurrected*, to be released in 2017.

Lorraine Fontana was raised in a working-class family in Queens, NY, and became a supporter of the civil rights and Black empowerment movements and an antiwar activist early in life. She joined VISTA in 1968, which brought her to Atlanta where she came out among other leftists and feminist women who together founded the ALFA. She later used her legal training at the People's College of Law at Georgia Legal Services, the EEOC, and the Lambda Legal Defense and Education Fund.

Martha Ingalls is a contemplative writer, photographer, and per-cussionist, and is a long-time student of metaphysics and spiritual teachings. A North Carolina native, Martha spend her formative lesbian years in South Florida's diverse lesbian community from 1982 to 1996. She currently resides in North Carolina but carries the spirits of her lesbian sisters from that time in her heart, always.

Merril Mushroom grew up in Miami Beach, FL, and came out there in the 1950s. She has been an activist and community organizer since the 1970s when she lived in New York City. In 1973, she moved to rural Middle Tennessee where she continues to misbehave. Her old-timey bar dyke stories can be found in out-of-print lesbian publications of the 1980s and 1990s.

Michele Crone has been a "bicoastal resident," but has voted in Provincetown, MA, for twenty years. There, she has provided venues for new artists while continuing to produce well-known performers like Holly Near, Lea DeLaria, Lucie Blue Tremblay, and Alix Dobkin. She advocates for Elders and persons with disabilities, and currently serves on a city commission reviewing the Provincetown town charter.

Molly Chadbourne lives in Chapel Hill, North Carolina, with her husband, dog, and sixteen chickens. She is a registered nurse and manages the Sexual Assault Nurse Examiner team for Duke Hospital in Durham, NC. She is studying to be a Family Nurse Practitioner at UNC-Chapel Hill School of Nursing. She continues to love women's music and has kept a Ladyslipper orchid growing in her home since 2007.

Phyllis Free, BFA, MLS, is an interdisciplinary artist-activist and professional drummer who incorporates her love of poetry, storytelling, music, drama, dance, and visual arts into theatrical ensemble productions, installations, exhibitions, workshops, residencies, publications, recordings, partnerships in community arts and education programs, and creative collaborations with other arts professionals. Contact for information: Phyllis Free/ Creative Services phylfree@mindspring.com. alternateroots.org/ tour/artists/phyllis_free 502/938-8427.

Rand Hall retired ten years ago as co-editor and publisher of *The Gazette, the Suncoast Gay and Lesbian News Magazine* in Florida. She moved to a lesbian community in rural Alabama. She is a writer, woman, mother, grandmother, former activist, very out lesbian, dyke, butch, artist, and lover. She has been writing since she was big enough to hold a pencil. Lesbian Space, and Womyn's Space have nurtured her and are precious to her. She has attended Womonwrites since 1979 when she was a baby dyke. Womonwriters are her tribe.

Robin Toler has a feminist therapy practice in Louisiana based on the principles of equity and human rights. She offers art therapy, addictions counseling, and trauma resolution. Toler plays shekere in Bloco Jacaré, a samba group. She enjoys art making, writing, traveling, and teaching. Contact her at www.robintoler.com and www.robintolerartstudio.com.

Rose Norman is a retired professor of English and women's studies who grew up in rural Alabama and now lives in Huntsville, Alabama. Her lifelong interest in stories of women's lives led to scholarly research on American women's autobiography. As general editor of the Southern Lesbian-Feminist Activist Herstory Project, she has interviewed eighty-seven lesbians, and is eager to interview more.

Sage Morse lives in St. Petersburg, FL, and teaches for the Hospital/Homebound Program of Pinellas County Schools. She currently sings with Crescendo, the Tampa Bay Women's Chorus, and is also the president. She is very active with the Teachers' Union (in a state which hates unions) and takes great pleasure in hassling the state legislators as a union rep. She was one of the contributors to and editors of *Womyn's Words* from 1982 until its final edition in 2010.

Sandra Tarlin is Associate Professor of English at Bronx Community College, CUNY. She received her PhD in English and Creative Writing from the University of Houston. Her poems have appeared in such journals as *Ark/angel Review*, *Bridges*, *Mobius*, *Poetica*, *Sinister Wisdom*, and *Western Humanities Review*.

Sue Massek has called Kentucky home for forty years and is deeply devoted to Appalachia and the people who live there. She has performed as a solo artist and as banjo player for The Reel World String Band since its beginning in 1977, using music as a tool for social justice in venues as diverse as community centers in the coal fields of Appalachia to Lincoln Center in New York City.

Woody Blue was born and raised in northeastern Ohio. She became involved in radical peace and lesbian politics during the 1980s at the Seneca Women's Peace Encampment and the National LGBT Marches in Washington, DC. She emigrated to the South in the 1990s, connecting with the Gainesville, FL, community. Since then she has come out as a massage therapist and textile artist, specializing in Peace Flags. She displays her work at Southern Pride Festivals and other hotspots.

FOR IMMEDIATE RELEASE:

Contact: Batya Weinbaum at femspec@aol.com

Get our new and back issues by paypal at **www.femspec.org**

16.2: *"Teaching and Learning about Feminist Speculative Arts in the Digital Age Issue" Volume (2016). Includes: Articles on* Teaching Feminism Online; *Historical Documents*

Intersection of Gender and Age in the Early Pulp Years of SF: Analysis and Story Abstracts

LESLIE F. STONE. The Fall of Mercury (excerpt)

Poetry by CONSTANCE BRERETON.

Book Reviews: MAIJA HATTON. Ruth B. Bottigheimer. *Fairy Tales Framed.* SUNY Press ALCENA ROGAN. Marleen S. Barr. *Oy Feminist Planets: A Fake Memoir*, NeoPoiesis Press Books and Media Received

17.1: (231 pp) contains a comprehensive index for our issues 1.1-16.1 prepared by a team of professional librarians; book reviews on women and war in textiles; women in ancient art; women in comedy; exhibit reviews of Leonora Carrington's retrospective in London and art of domestic abuse in southern CA; a personal reflection of Leonora Carrington by surrealist art critic Gloria Orenstein; an interview with Kate Millet; a critical article on late motherhood by Maria Aline Ferreira, "Monstrous Motherhood: Alternative Visions of Late Pregnancy."

Also **Femspec** Books and Productions Publishes *Toward Utopia: Feminist Dystopian Writing and Religious Fundamentalism in Margaret Atwood's* The Handmaid's Tale, *Louise Marley's* The Terrorists of Irustand, *and Marge Piercy's* He, She and It (Femspec Books, 2015) $24.95

Need professional development? *Femspec* needs you! Especially web skills needed, and ability to post past articles for individual sale on Smashwords....

Sinister Wisdom **Back Issues Available**

103 Celebrating the Michigan Womyn's Music Festival ($12)
102 The Complete Works of Pat Parker ($22.95)
101 Variations ($12)
100 Anniversary ($12)
99 Pleasure ($12)
98 Landykes of the South ($12)
97 Out Latina Lesbians ($12)
96 What Can I Ask ($18.95)
95 Reconciliations ($12)
94 Lesbians and Exile ($12)
93 Southern Lesbian-Feminist Herstory 1968–94 ($12)
92 Lesbian Healthcare Workers ($12)
91 Living as a Lesbian ($17.95)
90 Catch, Quench ($12)
89 Once and Later ($12)
88 Crime Against Nature ($17.95)
87 Tribute to Adrienne Rich
86 Ignite!
85 Youth/Humor
84 Time/Space
83 Identity and Desire
82 In Amerika They Call Us Dykes: Lesbian Lives in the 70s
81 Lesbian Poetry – When? And Now!
80 Willing Up and Keeling Over
78/79 Old Lesbians/Dykes II
77 Environmental Issues Lesbian Concerns
76 Open Issue
75 Lesbian Theories/Lesbian Controversies
74 Latina Lesbians
73 The Art Issue
72 Utopia
71 Open Issue
70 30th Anniversary Celebration
68/69 Death, Grief and Surviving
67 Lesbians and Work
66 Lesbians and Activism
65 Lesbian Mothers & Grandmothers
64 Lesbians and Music, Drama and Art
63 Lesbians and Nature
62 Lesbian Writers on Reading and Writing *
61 Women Loving Women in Prison
59/60 Love, Sex & Romance
58 Open Issue

57 Healing
55 Exploring Issues of Racial & Sexual Identification
54 Lesbians & Religion
53 Old Dykes/Lesbians – Guest Edited by Lesbians Over 60
52 Allies Issue
51 New Lesbian Writing
50 Not the Ethics Issue
49 The Lesbian Body
48 Lesbian Resistance Including work by Dykes in Prison
47 Lesbians of Color: Tellin' It Like It 'Tis
46 Dyke Lives
45 Lesbians & Class (the first issue of a lesbian journal edited entirely by poverty and working class dykes)
43/44 15th Anniversary double-size (368 pgs) retrospective
41 Italian American Women's Issue
40 Friendship
39 Disability
36 Surviving Psychiatric Assault/ Creating emotional well being
35 Passing
34 Sci-Fi, Fantasy & Lesbian Visions
33 Wisdom
32 Open Issue

*Available on audio tape

Back issues are $6.00 unless noted plus $3.00 Shipping & Handling for 1st issue; $1.00 for each additional issue. Order online at www.sinisterwisdom.org

Or mail check or money order to:
Sinister Wisdom
2333 McIntosh Road
Dover, FL 33527-5980